THE
WORDS
YOU
SHOULD
KNOW TO
SOUND
SMART

THE
WORDS
YOU
SHOULD
KNOW TO
SOUND
SMART

1,200 ESSENTIAL WORDS
EVERY SOPHISTICATED PERSON
SHOULD BE ABLE TO USE

ROBERT W. BLY

Aadamsmedia
Avon, Massachusetts

*"Having an extensive vocabulary is the fundamental
building block for thinking, communication, and learning. The better
you are able to think, communicate, and learn, the better your chances for success."*
—Celeste Stewart

Published by
Adams Media, a division of F+W Media, Inc.
57 Littlefield Street, Avon, MA 02322. U.S.A.
www.adamsmedia.com

ISBN 10: 1-59869-886-9
ISBN 13: 978-1-59869-886-2

Printed in the United States of America.

J I H G

Library of Congress Cataloging-in-Publication Data
is available from the publisher.

This publication is designed to provide accurate and authoritative information with
regard to the subject matter covered. It is sold with the understanding that the publisher is not engaged in rendering legal, accounting, or other professional advice. If
legal advice or other expert assistance is required, the services of a competent professional person should be sought.
    —From a *Declaration of Principles* jointly adopted by a Committee of the
American Bar Association and a Committee of Publishers and Associations

Many of the designations used by manufacturers and sellers to distinguish their
product are claimed as trademarks. Where those designations appear in this book
and Adams Media was aware of a trademark claim, the designations have been
printed with initial capital letters.

*This book is available at quantity discounts for bulk purchases.
For information, please call 1-800-289-0963.*

CONTENTS

Dedication   vi

Acknowledgments   vii

Introduction   viii

About the Author   237

Index   239

DEDICATION

For Peter Archer, a saint among men

ACKNOWLEDGMENTS

A prodigious debt of gratitude goes to Justin Cord Hayes and Katie Corcoran Lytle for the Herculean effort they put forth to ameliorate this book. Thanks also to the following friends, family, and colleagues who suggested words for inclusion in this book: Ilise Benun, Milly Bly, Fern Dickey, Amy and Jonathan Eiten, Don Hauptman, Ken and Teri Karp, Michael Masterson, and Mike Payntner.

INTRODUCTION

A Few Words about a Few Words

A radio commercial for a mail-order course on building your vocabulary states, "People judge you by the words you use." Now, with *The Words You Should Know to Sound Smart*, people who hear you speak will see you as smart—perhaps even smarter than you really are.

Some people who want to sound smart have cultivated a large vocabulary, which they unleash with great regularity. This book can serve as your "translator" when speaking with these pseudo-intellectuals.

Many other people possess a large vocabulary but use it sparingly, preferring to speak and write in plain English. As more than one writing instructor has put it, "Your goal is to express, not to impress."

It's possible that *The Words You Should Know to Sound Smart* may even put some money in your pocket. People who have a good vocabulary come off as confident, intelligent, and motivated—qualities necessary for financial success. The late motivational speaker Earl Nightingale liked to tell students about a twenty-year study of college graduates. The study concluded, "Without a single exception, those who had scored highest on the vocabulary test given in college were in the top income group, while those who had scored the lowest were in the bottom income group."

Scientist John O'Connor gave vocabulary tests to executive and supervisory personnel in thirty-nine large manufacturing companies. On average, test scores for the company presidents were nearly three times higher than their shop foremen. Vocabulary researchers Richard C. Anderson and W. E. Nagy write, "One of the most consistent findings of educational research is that having a small vocabulary portends poor school performance and, conversely, having a large vocabulary is associated with school success."

Whether this book helps you get higher grades or advance in your career, it's fun to improve your command of the English language—either to impress *or* express. Some of the words in *The Words You Should Know to Sound Smart* can do just that: make you sound educated and intelligent. But you may get pleasure out of knowing them and adding them to your vocabulary quiver, even if you keep most of them in reserve. It's your call.

A Note on the Pronunciation

Pronunciation keys given in this book are rendered phonetically, without using special symbols or systems.

Many of the words in this book have meanings and pronunciations—in addition to those listed here—that are entirely correct.

Regional influences can affect pronunciation of certain words. In this book, we use the most commonly accepted pronunciation for each word, recognizing that it is by no means the only acceptable pronunciation.

A Note on the Sources

In his book *The Meaning of Everything: The Story of the Oxford English Dictionary*, Simon Winchester observes that there are essentially three sources for the words in any dictionary: (1) words found in existing dictionaries; (2) words overheard in conversation; and (3) words found "by a concerted trawl through the text of literature." *The Words You Should Know to Sound Smart* is my attempt at a listing of all three sources.

"Of course the illusion of art is to make one believe that great literature is very close to life, but exactly the opposite is true. Life is AMORPHOUS, literature is formal."

Françoise Sagan, French novelist and playwright

abatement *(ah-BAIT-ment), noun*
The reduction or elimination of a tax, claim, fine, or debt.
> *By having her daddy pull strings in the mayor's office, Sylvia received a quick ABATEMENT of her traffic ticket.*

abjure *(ab-JOOR), transitive verb*
To renounce or turn your back on a belief or position you once held near and dear.
> *Once Jodi tasted my mouth-watering, medium-rare filet mignon, she ABJURED the vegetarian lifestyle forever.*

abominate *(uh-BOM-in-ate), verb*
When you *abominate* something, you really, really hate and dislike it – and view it with considerable loathing.
> *"For my part, I ABOMINATE all honorable respectable toils, trials, and tribulations of every kind whatsoever." – Herman Melville, American author*

abscond *(ab-SKOND), verb*
To leave in a hurry but quietly, so as to escape notice, especially to avoid trouble.
> *Bored out of his wits, Jared ABSCONDED with the family Mercedes, but he wrapped it around a large oak tree.*

abstemious *(ab-STEE-me-us), adjective*
To eat plain and simple food in moderation, avoiding over-indulgence in drink and gluttony at the table.
> *Gandhi led an ABSTEMIOUS life.*

abstruse *(ab-STROOS), adjective*
Arcane, complex, difficult to understand and learn.
> *Bob began to wish there was, in fact, a Santa Claus because he found the "simple instructions" to his son's bicycle far too ABSTRUSE.*

acculturation *(ah-kul-cherr-AYE-shin), noun*
The process of adapting to a different culture.
> *Just because sushi makes me queasy, doesn't mean I'm opposed to ACCULTURATION.*

acrimonious *(ah-kri-MOAN-ee-us), adjective*
Angry; bitter; disputed.

"There is something about the literary life that repels me, all this desperate building of castles on cobwebs, the long-drawn **ACRIMONIOUS** struggle to make something important which we all know will be gone forever in a few years . . ." – *Raymond Chandler, American author*

A

adjudicate *(ah-JOO-dih-kate), verb*
To preside over or listen to opposing arguments and help two parties settle their difference and come to an agreement.

As my daughters pummeled each other while screaming at top volume, I tried desperately to ADJUDICATE their quarrel.

ad nauseam *(ad-NAW-zee-um), adverb*
Something that goes on and on, or is done over and over again, to a ridiculous, even sickening degree.

At first we were all impressed that Steve could recite the entire Gettysburg Address, but we all got kind of sickened when he repeated the feat AD NAUSEAM.

adroit *(ah-DROYT), adjective*
Skilled or clever in a particular pursuit.

"It's kind of sad," Betty said to Barbara, "that Will thinks his ADROIT opera-singing abilities will impress women."

adulatory *(ad-JYOO-lah-tore-ee), adjective*
Complimentary; giving of effusive praise.

"He includes in his final chapter a passage of ADULATORY prose from Henry James." – Joyce Carol Oates, American author

aegis *(AYE-jis), noun*
The protection, support, and help rendered by a guardian, supporter, backer, or mentor.

Jill thinks she's above reproach because she's under the AEGIS of that marketing vice-president with a penchant for younger women.

aesthetic *(es-THEH-tik), adjective*
Relating to beauty and the appreciation of beauty.

Covering your walls with pictures torn from the newspaper does not constitute a genuine AESTHETIC sense, Harold.

affectation *(ah-fek-TAY-shun), noun*
Behaviors or mannerisms that are exaggerated, extreme, eccentric, and deliberately showy, often an effort to attract attention.
> *"AFFECTATION is awkward and forces imitation of what should be genuine and easy." – John Locke, British philosopher*

afflatus *(uh-FLAY-tuss), noun*
Inspiration that seems to come from divine origin.
> *The Nobel Prize-winning novelist attributed her abilities to AFFLATUS, rather than to her own abilities.*

aficionado *(uh-fish-ee-uh-NAH-doe), noun*
A devotee, someone who is enthralled with and supports a particular activity.
> *Dwight often refers to himself as an AFICIONADO of American-made microbrews.*

aggrandize *(ah-GRAND-ize), verb*
To exaggerate, put on a false front, and make something look greater and grander than it really is.
> *Phil tries to AGGRANDIZE his reputation by stating that he is a charter member of the Bill O'Reilly fan club, but everybody just thinks this "feat" makes him pathetic.*

akimbo *(ah-KIM-bo), adverb*
With hands on hips and elbows turned outward.
> *When my father gets really mad, he stands stock-still, arms AKIMBO, and slowly turns red in the face.*

alacrity *(ah-LAK-rih-tee), noun*
Cheerful cooperation rendered with enthusiasm, promptness, and politeness.
> *The ALACRITY with which Steve responded to Helen's invitation is nothing short of astonishing.*

albeit *(al-BEE-it), conjunction*
Though.
> *Vickie thought Charles was dim-witted, ALBEIT cute, in a childlike way.*

aleatory *(AIL-ee-ah-tore-ee), adjective*
An action that is unplanned, spontaneous, or spur of the moment rather than deliberately thought out and carefully considered; an outcome that is anything but certain and depends on luck, randomness, or chance.

"Of course you lost the election!" Miranda yelled. "An ALEATORY, fly-by-the-seat-of-your-pants campaign is never going to be a recipe for success!"

allegory *(AL-eh-gor-ee), noun*
A story told to communicate a hidden meaning or deeper theme.
Many of the Grimm Brothers' fairy tales are clear ALLEGORIES of the consequences of children's rotten behavior.

alliteration *(ah-lit-ter-AYE-shun), noun*
The repetition of similar sounds, especially at the beginnings of words, in written speech or the spoken word.
I'd forgotten how much Alicia likes to use ALLITERATION in her insults, but was quickly reminded when she called me a cruel, callous cretin.

amatory *(AM-uh-tore-ee), adjective*
Having to do with sexual love.
Pete hasn't stopped sulking since Alice spurned his AMATORY advances at the office Christmas party.

ambiguity *(am-bih-GYOO-ih-tee), noun*
Uncertainty; lacking clear definition.
Poets who revel in AMBIGUITY are one of the reasons many people hate poetry.

ameliorate *(ah-MEAL-your-ate), verb*
To correct a deficiency or defect; to make right a wrong; to take actions that make up, at least in part, for negative actions or failure to take action previously.
After you insulted her mother, I don't think even the most expensive piece of jewelry will be enough to AMELIORATE your relationship with Marcia.

amenable *(ah-MEE-nah-bull), adjective*
One who readily and agreeably gives in to the wishes and desires of others.
Mark considers himself AMENABLE, but the rest of us just think he's a pushover.

amorphous *(ah-MORE-fis), adjective*
Without definite shape, substance, or form; lacking definition and boundaries.

"Of course the illusion of art is to make one believe that great literature is very close to life, but exactly the opposite is true. Life is AMORPHOUS, literature is formal." – Françoise Sagan, French novelist and playwright

anachronism *(ah-NAK-ruh-niz-em), noun*
A person, place, thing, or idea whose time is past, and that seems to belong to an earlier age.
> *His three record players—and the fact that he doesn't even know what an mp3 is—make Jim something of an ANACHRONISM.*

analogous *(an-AL-a-gus), adjective*
Similar or comparable in some respects.
> *Nikki tried to argue that attending public school in Manhattan was ANALOGOUS to attending the prestigious boarding school in the country, but her argument was weak and her grandmother wasn't buying it.*

anathema *(ah-NA-theh-MA), noun*
Something so distasteful to you, so alien and foreign to your understanding, that you find it sickening and repellant—as if you were allergic to it.
> *Religious services were an ANATHEMA to Russ, what with him being a dedicated atheist and all.*

androcentrism *(an-druh-SEN-tri-zum), noun*
An outlook that emphasizes a masculine point of view.
> *"Larry," Joan warned, "that ANDROCENTRISM may be all the rage in the locker room, but you'd better leave it out of our bedroom if you know what's good for you."*

androgynous *(ann-DRAH-gen-us), adjective*
Something or someone who is neuter—sexless; of indeterminate sex; or hermaphrodite (having characteristics of both a male and a female).
> *The models at fashion week were so ANDROGYNOUS that Katherine couldn't tell if the clothes were designed for men or women.*

anfractuous *(an-FRACK-chuh-wuss), adjective*
Full of windings and intricacies, like a good mystery novel.
> *The novel's ANFRACTUOUS plot worked on paper, but it became stupefyingly confusing—actually, just plain stupid—onscreen.*

animadversion *(an-uh-mad-VER-zhun), noun*
Very harsh criticism that suggests disapproval of what is being criticized.
> *My boss's frequent ANIMADVERSIONS have led to high staff turnover.*

anomaly *(an-AHM-ah-lee), noun*
An exception to the norm; something different and unexpected that logically should not exist.

> *"After a thousand meters of this broken-field walking, Mitsuno came upon an ANOMALY: a patch of sand perhaps ten meters square." – Fred Pohl and Thomas Thomas, American science fiction authors*

antecedent *(an-tih-SEE-dent), noun*
The ancestor of an existing product, idea, etc.

> *IBM's electronic typewriter with storage was the ANTECEDENT of the modern PC.*

antidisestablishmentarianism *(ant-eye-dis-es-STAB-lish-men-tarry-an-izm), noun*
A movement or protest against an established institution or authority.

> *No, Walter, bringing your own coffee to Starbuck's is not an example of ANTIDISESTABLISHMENTARIANISM. It's just foolish.*

antithesis *(an-TIH-thess-iss), noun*
The exact opposite; a thing that is completely different from another thing.

> *He tries so hard to be smooth, but Charles is the ANTITHESIS of cool.*

apartheid *(ah-PAR-thide), noun*
South Africa's government-sanctioned policy of segregation and racial discrimination.

> *Since APARTHEID ended in 1994, South Africa has elected three native African presidents.*

aphorism *(AH-for-iz-ihm), noun*
A proverb, often-repeated statement, or cliché.

> *Danny, you say "I'm right. You're wrong." so much that it's become an APHORISM.*

apocryphal *(ah-POCK-rih-full), adjective*
An event, story, legend, or rumor that has been told so often, and so long after the fact, that one has good reason to doubt its authenticity, nor can it be verified through research.

> *John Henry may have been based on a real man, but in the story he has grown to APOCRYPHAL proportions.*

apoplectic *(ap-up-PLECK-tic), adjective*
An extremely agitated state of rage.

Emily's careless event planning makes me so APOPLECTIC that I just want to step in and plan the luncheon myself.

apostasy *(a-PA-stah-see), noun*
The act of abandoning, ignoring, or openly flaunting an accepted principle or belief.
"It was his idea of grand APOSTASY to drive to the reform synagogue on the high holidays and park his pink-eye nag among the luxurious, whirl-wired touring cars of the rich." – Saul Bellow, American author

apotheosis *(ah-pa-thee-OH-sis), noun*
The culmination or highest point.
Winning the Silver Gutter Award at his local bowling alley was the APOTHEOSIS of Wendell's less-than-stellar sports legacy.

appeasement *(ah-PEEZ-meant), noun*
The act of making others happy by agreeing to their demands.
Charlene realized too late that her policy of APPEASEMENT would not cause Warren to treat her with more respect.

appelation *(ah-pull-AYE-shun), noun*
A formal name, label, or title.
Even though he has only an honorary degree, he insists on being called by the APPELLATION of "doctor" everywhere he goes.

approbation *(ap-ruh-BAY-shun), noun*
Official approval or commendation.
"In a virtuous and free state, no rewards can be so pleasing to sensible minds, as those which include the APPROBATION of our fellow citizens. My great pain is, lest my poor endeavours should fall short of the kind expectations of my country." – Thomas Jefferson

apropos *(ah-pro-POE), adverb*
Appropriate, or at an opportune time.
Charlie began screaming the words "Too late! Too late!" APROPOS of nothing.

arcane *(are-CAYNE), adjective*
Strange and mysterious; understood by only a few.
Bill's ARCANE knowledge of all Lexus models and their accessories is just a waste of gray matter.

archetype *(ARE-ke-type), noun*
A prototypical example; a recurrent theme or pattern; an original model that is widely imitated.

> *Boys never played with dolls until G.I. Joe became the ARCHETYPE of the "action figure."*

A

argosy *(are-guh-SEE), noun*
A rich, seemingly endless, supply.

> *The deceased hermit's home turned out to be an ARGOSY of Cuban cigars, Swiss timepieces, and historical erotica.*

artifice *(ARE-ti-fis), noun*
The use of clever strategies and cunning methods to fool or best others and tip an outcome in your favor.

> "Every art and **ARTIFICE** has been practiced and perpetrated to destroy the rights of man." – *Robert Ingersoll, American orator*

ascetic *(uh-SET-ik), noun*
A person who deliberately chooses to live a plain and simple life; characterized by lack of material possessions and strong self-discipline in all matters of behavior.

> *When Steve Jobs started Apple, a magazine profile portrayed him as an ASCETIC, noting that he had no furniture in his apartment.*

asperity *(a-SPARE-ih-tee), noun*
Something hard to endure.

> *Sorry, I can't handle the ASPERITY of a ballet. Could we watch football instead?*

assiduously *(ah-SID-you-us-lee), adverb*
Diligent and persistent, especially in an effort to help others, achieve a goal, or deliver on one's promises.

> *David worked ASSIDUOUSLY to complete his first novel, writing for three hours a night after work and dinner.*

assuage *(ah-SWAYJ), verb*
To put someone at ease; to comfort or soothe; to erase doubts and fears.

> *"But history must not yet tell the tragedies enacted here; let time intervene in some measure to ASSUAGE and lend an azure tint to them." – Henry David Thoreau, American author and transcendentalist*

asunder *(ah-SUN-derr), adjective*
A whole that has been split into parts; a union that has been eliminated, leaving the people or things once joined now separate.

> *His marriage torn ASUNDER, Mike decided to quit his job, move to Tangiers, and become a year-round beach bum.*

asynchronous *(aye-SINK-crow-nuss), adjective*
Acting or functioning with no regularity or discernible time schedule.

> *Maggie's ASYNCHRONOUS habits drive her friends crazy because they can never make advance plans with her.*

augur *(AW-ger), verb*
To predict or foretell the future.

> *The three witches of Shakespeare's* Macbeth *AUGUR the cataclysmic fate of the play's titular character.*

auspicious *(awe-SPIH-shus), adjective*
A good beginning giving rise to the belief that the venture, journey, or activity will end in success.

> *The blind date did not have an AUSPICIOUS start because Max kept calling his friend's cousin "Mallory" instead of "Mary."*

austere *(aw-STEER), adjective*
Stern; grim and lacking humor or warmth; clean and unornamented; severe or strict in manner.

> *In the movie* Dead Poets Society, *Robin Williams clashes with an AUSTERE headmaster at a private boy's school.*

autodidact *(AW-toe-dih-dakt), noun*
A self-educated person.

> *In the twentieth century, the library was the university of the AUTODIDACT; in the twenty-first century, it is the Internet.*

autonomy *(aw-THAN-ah-mee), noun*
Maintaining independent thought and action; free; self-governing; without dependence on, or under control of, a higher authority.

> *Herb claims he wants AUTONOMY, but he goes absolutely nuts whenever his boss gives him unstructured assignments.*

avant-garde *(AH-vant-GARD), noun, adjective*
New and experimental; especially referring to art, writing, architecture, and music.

"AVANT-GARDE art jousts with propriety, but takes care never to unseat." – Mason Cooley, American aphorist

avarice *(AH-ver-iss), noun*
The insatiable desire to have a lot of money, greed.
 "What you call AVARICE," Mary said, "I just call getting my share."

aver *(uh-VER), verb*
To assert the truthfulness of a statement.

> "'Has she no faults, then (Envy says), sir?' / Yes, she has one, I must **AVER**: / When all the world conspires to praise her, / The woman's deaf, and does not hear." – *Alexander Pope, British poet*

avuncular *(a-VUN-cue-lar), adjective*
Kind, genial, benevolent, like an uncle.
 Myron's AVUNCULAR personality makes women think of him as a friend, not as a lover.

axiom *(AKS-e-um), noun*
A truth or fact that is seen as self-evident, leaving no room for question or debate.
 Much to the chagrin of his creditors, Max adopted the AXIOM of those who have amassed great wealth: "Pay yourself first."

"A woman moved is like a fountain troubled. / Muddy, ill-seeming, thick, BEREFT of beauty, / And while it is so, none so dry or thirsty / Will deign to sip or touch one drop of it."

William Shakespeare

bacchanal *(bah-kan-AL), noun*
A wild celebration; a party at which the partygoers are loud and out of control, often fueled by excess alcohol consumption.

The initiation ceremony at the fraternity turned into a full-blown BAC-CHANAL requiring the intervention of the campus police to restore order.

badinage *(BAH-dih-nadge), noun*
Light, good-natured, even playful banter.

"If you don't care for me, you can move out now. I'm frankly not up to BADINAGE." – Harlan Ellison, American author

bailiwick *(BALE-ee-wick), noun*
A person's specific area of expertise, experience, skill, knowledge, education, or authority.

Foreign language is not my BAILIWICK, I soon realized after failing out of Hebrew School.

basilisk *(BAH-sill-isk), noun*
A mythical reptile with a lethal stare or breath.

With poisonous saliva that can kill a man with one bite, the Komodo Dragon is truly a modern-day BASILISK.

bastion *(BAS-tee-uhn), noun*
An institution, individual, or something else protecting or preserving a particular way of life, society, set of beliefs, or moral code.

Cliff, a Yale BASTION, continuously quibbles with Irene, who graduated summa cum laude from Harvard.

bathos *(BAY-thoss), noun*
A sudden change in mood from the solemn and serious to a more light-hearted, relaxed, and humorous outlook.

When the clock ticked at midnight on December 31, 1999, and we moved into the new century without the computers shutting down, the grim look and worried faces disappeared, and the IT department was suddenly enveloped in a feeling of BATHOS.

beatitude *(bee-AT-it-tood), noun*
Being in the highest possible state of happiness, good humor, and contentment.

"Kindness is a virtue neither modern nor urban. One almost unlearns it in a city. Towns have their own BEATITUDE; they are not unfriendly;

they offer a vast and solacing anonymity or an equally vast and solacing gregariousness." – Phyllis McGinley, American author and poet

beguiling *(bee-GUY-ling), adjective*
Charming; bewitching; enchanting.
The BEGUILING charm Monica learned at finishing school more than makes up for her vapid personality.

beleaguer *(beh-LEE-gir), verb*
To persistently surround, harass, or pester until you get what you want.
To the embarrassment of her friends, Kristen BELEAGUERED the sommelier until he brought her a satisfactory Bordeaux.

belie *(bee-LYE), verb*
To contradict or misrepresent.
Luther's mild-mannered, almost sickly appearance BELIED his physical conditioning and surprising strength.

belles lettres *(BELL-LET-truh), noun*
Novels, short stories, poems, and other writings read for their grace and literary style and not necessarily their content.

> "Learning has been as great a Loser by being … secluded from the World and good Company. By that Means, every Thing of what we call **BELLES LETTRES** became totally barbarous, being cultivated by Men without any Taste of Life or Manners." – **David Hume, Scottish philosopher**

bellicose *(BELL-ih-kose), adjective*
Belligerent, surly, ready to argue or fight at the slightest provocation.
Doug is so touchy about his new Jaguar that he'll instantly grow BELLICOSE if you so much as brush against it.

bellwether *(BELL-weather), noun*
A leading indicator or factor in determining a course of action or outcome.
The fact that Robert got thrown out of Groton and Exeter was a BELLWETHER for his lackadaisical years at Dartmouth.

beneficent *(be-NE-fih-sent), adjective*
Kindly in action, purpose, or speech.
In a BENEFICENT gesture, the neighborhood raised $10,000 to help pay for the young boy's leukemia treatments.

benighted *(bee-NYE-ted), adjective*
To be lost, ignorant, or unenlightened.
The Medieval period was a BENIGHTED era of superstition.

benign *(beh-NINE), adjective*
Kindly, gentle, generous of spirit, not harmful.
We thought Amanda BENIGN until she began to inflate her family pedigree.

bereaved *(beh-REEVD), adjective*
To be in a state of grief as the result of the death of someone you love or care deeply about.

"Laughter would be **BEREAVED** if snobbery died." – **Peter Ustinov, British writer and dramatist**

bereft *(Beh-REFT), adjective*
Lacking a certain characteristic, possession, or trait; isolated and lonely.
"A woman moved is like a fountain troubled. / Muddy, ill-seeming, thick, BEREFT of beauty, / And while it is so, none so dry or thirsty / Will deign to sip or touch one drop of it." – William Shakespeare

besotted *(bih-SOTT-ed), adjective*
Made foolish, stupid, or dull due to an infatuation with love, money, the pursuit of power, etc.
Aline thinks Jake is BESOTTED with her, but he's really BESOTTED with her father's stock portfolio.

bespoke *(bih-SPOHK), adjective*
Clothes, shoes, and other goods custom-made for a particular client.
Taylor's big secret is that though he wears BESPOKE clothing, he's only leasing his new Lexus.

bête noire *(Bett-NWAR), noun*
A thing for which one has an intense dislike or great fear; a dreaded enemy or foe.
Sunlight was Dracula's greatest BÊTE NOIRE.

betoken *(bee-TOE-ken), verb*
To serve as a warning.

For Mary and Paul, the breakdown of their new Porsche while they were still two hours away from their summer home BETOKENED a disastrous vacation.

bibelot *(BIB-low), noun*
A small object of beauty or rarity.
The Rossington's collection of BIBELOTS contains numerous Faberge eggs.

bibliomania *(bib-lee-oh-MAY-nee-uh), noun*
A preoccupation with the acquisition and ownership of books.
Lauren's BIBLIOMANIA extends only to her stockpile of catalogues for exclusive shops.

bibulous *(BIB-yuh-luss), adjective*
Related to drinking or to drunkenness.
Arthur thinks he's "fine," but his BIBULOUS activities are causing the club to consider permanent expulsion.

bicameral *(by-KAM-er-el), adjective*
A government or parliament with two chambers or houses.
With a Senate and a House of Representatives, the United States has a BICAMERAL legislature.

bifurcate *(BYE-fur-kate), verb*
To divide something into two branches or forks.
"François Truffaut defined a great movie as a perfect blend of truth and spectacle. Now it's become BIFURCATED. Studio films are all spectacle and no truth, and independent films are all truth and no spectacle." – Howard Franklin, American screenwriter and director

bilateral *(by-LAT-ur-ul), adjective*
Touching, existing on, or having or being agreed to by two sides.
The president signed a BILATERAL disarmament agreement with the nation bordering to the north.

bildungsroman *(BILL-dungs-roh-man), noun*
A coming-of-age novel, such as *The Catcher in the Rye* or *A Portrait of the Artist as a Young Man*.
Alex has started writing a BILDUNGSROMAN about his experiences in prep school.

bilious *(BILL-yuss), adjective*
Having a nasty temperament or disagreeable disposition; to be "full of bile" and hatred.
> *The polo team's BILIOUS captain made his team miserable as he proceeded to criticize their every move.*

billet *(BILL-uht), noun*
A job, position, or appointment.
> *With his wealthy father's influence, Miles was able to secure a lucrative BILLET in a major brokerage house.*

blandishments *(BLAN-dish-ments), noun*
Compliments rendered primarily to influence and gain favor with the person you are praising.
> *The BLANDISHMENTS heaped upon the consultant by his client were not sufficient to persuade him to take a staff position with them.*

blazon *(BLAY-zuhn), noun or verb*
A coat of arms; or, to proclaim something widely.
> *You'll find the Rutherford's family BLAZON on every one of Prescott's ties.*

bloviate *(BLOH-vee-ayt), verb*
To speak pompously and at length
> *Maxwell BLOVIATES about his "excellent" golf game, but everyone knows he inflates his handicap exponentially.*

bona fide *(BO-nah-fyed), adjective*
Legitimate, the real thing, the genuine article.
> *He may not come across as particularly intelligent, but Brian's Phi Beta Kappa key is, in fact, BONA FIDE.*

bonhomie *(bon-uh-MEE), noun*
A good-natured, genial manner.
> *Even though he has no family pedigree, Walker is accepted into our group because of his contagious BONHOMIE.*

bourgeois *(boor-ZHWAH), adjective*
Pertaining or relating to the middle class, as opposed to the upper class or royalty on one end and the peasants or common laborers on the other.
> *"The representation of the garrison thus turned out to be incomparably more moderate and BOURGEOIS than the soldier masses." – Leon Trotsky, Bolshevik revolutionary and Marxist theorist*

bovine *(BO-vyne), adjective*
Anything related to or reminiscent of cows or other dull, docile, slow-moving, grazing mammals.

> "The cow is of the **BOVINE** ilk; One end is moo, the other, milk." – *Ogden Nash, American poet*

bowdlerize *(BOWED-ler-eyes), verb*
To remove obscenity, violence, and other inappropriate content from a novel, play, or story so as to make it appropriate for a younger reader.
> *Hollywood BOWDLERIZED his script so, instead of being R-rated, the film was rated PG-13.*

braggadocio *(brag-uh-DOH-see-oh), noun*
Empty boasting or bragging.
> *Eric claims he is a consummate wine connoisseur, but it is just BRAGGADOCIO.*

breviary *(BREE-vee-air-ee), noun*
A brief summary or abridgement.
> *She called it a BREVIARY, but Lana's recounting of her family's month on the Riviera was anything but short.*

Brobdingnagian *(brahb-ding-NAG-ian), adjective*
Describes a thing or person of enormous size; huge.
> *Andre the Giant was a man of BROBDINGNAGIAN proportions, standing seven-foot-five-inches and weighing over 500 pounds.*

brouhaha *(BREW-ha-ha), noun*
A confusing, exciting, and turmoil-rife event.
> *Madeline caused a BROUHAHA when she told her parents she was eschewing Harvard for a state school in order to be closer to her boyfriend.*

bromide *(BRO-mide), noun*
A cliché or tired saying used to express an idea without any thought or originality.
> *Helen's Harvard education does not stop her from peppering her speech with insipid BROMIDES.*

brummagem *(BRUHM-uh-juhm), noun or adjective*
Describes something that looks great but performs poorly.
> *"Our press is certainly bankrupt in . . . reverence for nickel plate and brummagem." – Mark Twain*

bucolic *(byoo-KOL-ick), adjective*
A peaceful, serene, rural object, place, or environment.
> *We bought a weekend place in a BUCOLIC little village in the country.*

bugaboo *(BUHG-uh-boo), noun*
Something that causes fear and worry, often needlessly.
> *Angela caused a BUGABOO when she informed her family that she was leaving the Episcopal Church.*

bulwark *(bull-WARK), noun*
A defensive, protective barrier, wall, or force.

> "Since he aims at great souls, he cannot miss. But if someone should slander me in this way, no one would believe him. For envy goes against the powerful. Yet slight men, apart from the great, are but a weak **BULWARK**." *– Sophocles, Greek tragedian*

bumptious *(BUMP-shuss), adjective*
Loud and assertive in a crude way.
> *The club's golf pro was fired due to his BUMPTIOUS behavior on the links.*

burgeon *(BURR-jin), verb*
To sprout, to grow; to blossom and flourish.
> *Natalia does her part for the BURGEONING "green" movement by having her gardener turn manure from her stables into fertilizer.*

byzantine *(biz-ann-TEEN), adjective*
A convoluted plan; a scheme that is overly complicated; a puzzle or task that's difficult to figure out because of its complexity.
> *We found it impossible to follow the BYZANTINE plot of how Eileen made Mariah a laughingstock by replacing her Prada shoes with nearly identical knockoffs.*

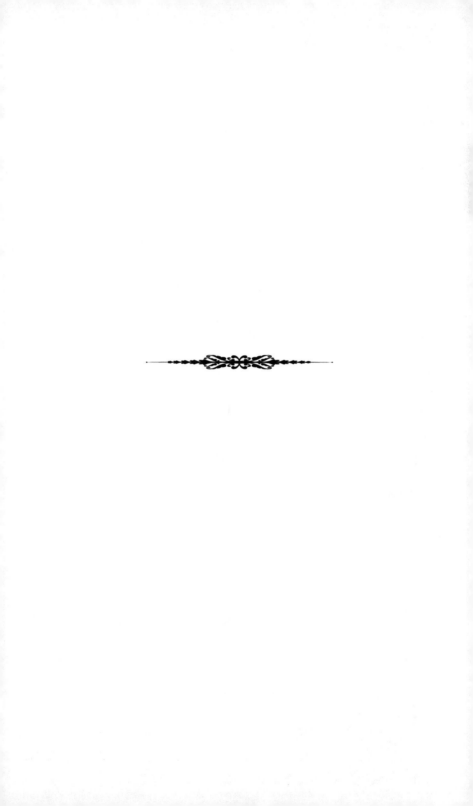

*"We romped until the pans /
Slid from the kitchen shelf; / My
mother's COUNTENANCE /
Could not unfrown itself."*

———

Theodore Roethke, American poet

cabal *(kah-BAHL), noun*
An underground society, secret religious sect, or other private group assembled for purposes hidden from those around them.
> *I was shocked when our neighbor asked us to join a CABAL of devil worshippers; after all, he is a deacon at the local church!*

cabotage *(KAB-uh-tij), noun*
The right of a country to control all air traffic flying in its skies.
> *After 9/11, CABOTAGE became a major concern of New York City and its mayor.*

cache *(KASH), noun*
Something hidden or stored.
> *Everyone was jealous when they learned of Moira's CACHE of acceptances to the finest schools.*

caducous *(kuh-DOO-kuss), adjective*
Transitory; short-lived; perishable.
> *"Some thing, which I fancied was a part of me, falls off from me and leaves no scar. It was CADUCOUS." – Ralph Waldo Emerson, American poet, essayist, and transcendentalist*

calumny *(KAL-um-nee), noun*
The act of libel or slander; to besmirch a person's reputation by spreading false statements and rumors.
> *"CALUMNY will sear virtue itself." –William Shakespeare*

cannonade *(CAN-non-ayd), noun*
A continuous, relentless bombardment or effort.
> *A CANNONADE of questioning greeted Eva's statement that she was quitting the club's tennis team.*

capacious *(kuh-PAY-shus), adjective*
A huge open space; roomy; a large interior or room.
> *All of our meetings take place in the golf club's CAPACIOUS private auditorium.*

capitulation *(kah-pih-chew-LAY-shun), noun*
The act of surrendering or giving up.
> *Ross offered James no CAPITULATION during the confrontational lacrosse game.*

capricious *(kah-PREE-shus), adjective*
Prone to quickly change one's mind, decision, or course of action at the drop of a hat or on impulse.
> *"I do not understand the CAPRICIOUS lewdness of the sleeping mind."*
> *– John Cheever, American novelist*

captious *(KAP-shuss), adjective*
A person who enjoys giving unsolicited advice; a nitpicker; a petty individual who takes pleasure in pointing out the flaws in and mistakes made by others, no matter how small.
> *Audrey is a CAPTIOUS individual eager to show others how smart she is, often by belittling them.*

carouse *(kuh-ROWZ), verb*
To engage in boisterous social activity.
> *We CAROUSED until dawn at the annual New Year's Eve party that the Weatherton's hold on their yacht.*

castigate *(KAS-tuh-gate), verb*
To scold or criticize harshly, with the objective of assigning blame and motivating the other person to correct their error.
> *The bartender was CASTIGATED by his boss for serving alcohol to two teenage girls without checking their ID first.*

catharsis *(kah-THAR-sis), noun*
The purging of the senses through tragic drama or through music; or, in general, a discharge of negative emotions.
> *After losing matches at the club's courts, Puccini's* Madama Butterfly *always leads Celeste to CATHARSIS.*

caveat *(KAV-ee-ott), noun*
A precaution or warning.
> *Before Arthur applied to college, his sister offered him a CAVEAT: "Many of us do not consider Columbia to be a true Ivy League school."*

chimera *(kih-MER-ah), noun*
An object, place, event, or combination of things so strange, odd, and improbable that it logically should not exist in the real world—and yet, it does.
> *"What a CHIMERA then is humankind. What a novelty! What a monster, what a chaos!" – Blaise Pascal, French philosopher*

chivalry *(SHIV-ul-ree)*, *noun*
Brave, kind, courteous, or gentlemanly behavior.
> *"We hear much of CHIVALRY of men towards women; but . . . it vanishes like dew before the summer sun when one of us comes into competition with the manly sex." – Martha Coston, American author*

cholers *(KOH-lers)*, *noun*
The mood of anger, irritability, grumpiness, or being short-tempered and impatient.
> *When Franklin is in the grip of CHOLERS, even his closest friends avoid his table at the club.*

circuitous *(sir-CUE-uh-tuss)*, *adjective*
Extremely twisty and winding; indirect.
> *Blanche called it a shortcut, but her CIRCUITOUS directions caused us to arrive very late at the debutante ball.*

circumlocution *(sir-kum-low-CUE-shun)*, *noun*
Language that is pompous, overly formal, wordy, and redundant.
> *Grant used CIRCUMLOCUTION to suggest that he attended a prep school, but all of us know he is a product of public education.*

circumspect *(SIR-kum-spekt)*, *adjective*
Prudent, cautious, and well considered.

> "I smiled, / I waited, / I was **CIRCUMSPECT**; / O never, never, never write that I / missed life or loving." – *Hilda Doolittle, American poet and memoirist*

clandestine *(klan-DES-tyne)*, *adjective*
Refers to activities that are secret, covert, and perhaps not fully authorized or sanctioned.
> *"CLANDESTINE steps upon imagined stairs / Climb through the night, because his cuckoos call." – Wallace Stevens, American poet*

clarion *(KLAR-ee-uhn)*, *adjective*
Clear and shrill, like sound.
> *On the day classes began at his prep school, Paul groaned at the CLARION call of his morning alarm.*

cloying *(KLOYE-ing), adjective*
Sickeningly sweet, sappy, or sentimental.
> *"Minerva save us from the CLOYING syrup of coercive compassion!"*
> *– Camille Paglia, American author, feminist, and social critic*

codify *(KAHD-uh-fye), verb*
To organize into a system of rules, codes, or principles; to make clear and coherent.
> *Fiona set out to CODIFY the rules associated with her exclusive clique.*

cogent *(KOH-gent), adjective*
A case or argument presented in a reasoned, well-thought-out, logical, compelling, and persuasive manner.
> *Corey offered a very COGENT argument in favor of insider trading.*

cognizant *(KOG-nih-sint), adjective*
Aware of the realities of a situation.
> *Amanda is always COGNIZANT of her acquaintances' pedigrees.*

cognoscente *(kon-yuh-SHEN-tee), noun*
Person with superior knowledge or understanding of a particular field.
> *As a result of my many years living in the Bordeaux region of France, I am very much a COGNOSCENTE of wine and winemaking.*

colloquial *(kah-LOW-kwee-ul), adjective*
Informal, conversational, everyday language.

> **"COLLOQUIAL** poetry is to the real art as the barber's wax dummy is to sculpture." – *Ezra Pound, American expatriate poet*

commodious *(kah-MOW-dee-us), adjective*
Very spacious.
> *Though COMMODIOUS, the Barrows' Cape Cod home is austere and lacks charm.*

compendious *(kuhm-PEN-dee-us), adjective*
Concise, succinct; to the point.
> *Sheila is unable to tell COMPENDIOUS stories about her trips to the Riviera.*

complaisant *(kuhm-PLAY-zuhnt), adjective*
Agreeable and eager to please.
> *Eleanor is far too COMPLAISANT with common strangers.*

comport *(kum-PORT), verb*
To conduct oneself; to behave in a particular way.
> *Roger always embarrasses us because he seems to think his family name frees him to COMPORT himself foolishly.*

compunction *(kuhm-PUHNGK-shun), noun*
Anxiety caused by regret for doing another harm.
> *Thomas never feels COMPUNCTION for the bruises he leaves on the lacrosse field.*

compurgation *(kom-purr-GAY-shun), noun*
A practice by which an accused person can be found not guilty if twelve or more people take an oath testifying to the validity of his claim of innocence.
> *The Anglo-Saxon process of COMPURGATION is the basis of the modern American jury system.*

conciliatory *(kon-SILL-ee-ah-tore-ee), adjective*
Actions or words meant to settle a dispute or resolve a conflict in a manner that leaves no hard feelings on either side.
> *"If you are not very clever, you should be CONCILIATORY." – Benjamin Disraeli, British statesmen and literary figure*

concomitant *(KON-koh-mit-ant), noun*
Something that exists or occurs with something else.
> *"Each action of the actor on the stage should be the visible CONCOMITANT of his thoughts." – Sarah Bernhardt, nineteenth-century French actress and author*

concupiscence *(kon-KYOO-pih-suhns), noun*
Unbridled lust in the extreme—horniness.
> *"You're talking to a young vampire, a fountain of CONCUPISCENCE." – Mario Acevedo, American fantasy author*

confabulate *(kuhn-FAB-yuh-late), verb*
To chat or converse informally.
> *Jarod proceeded to CONFABULATE about the wines most recently added to the family cellar.*

consecrate *(KON-seh-krayt), verb*
To declare something sacred, true, sacrosanct, or involuble.
> *"It is regarded as normal to CONSECRATE virginity in general and to lust for its destruction in particular." – Karl Kraus, Austrian writer*

consummate *(KON-suh-mitt), adjective*
Complete or perfect; showing supreme skill.
> *"[John F. Kennedy is] a new star with a tremendous national appeal, the skill of a CONSUMMATE showman." – Russell Baker, American author*

contiguous *(kon-TIG-yew-us), adjective*
Adjacent; sharing a common border; sitting next to one another in a row or sequence.
> *The network extends to the forty-eight CONTIGUOUS states.*

contretemps *(KON-truh-tahn), noun*
An inopportune occurrence with embarrassing results.
> *"Pan had been amongst them . . .the little god Pan, who presides over social CONTRETEMPS and unsuccessful picnics." – E. M. Forster, English novelist*

conundrum *(kuh-NUN-drum), noun*
A difficult problem or situation that is not easily resolved.
> *Knowing whether to attend MIT, Yale, or Harvard was quite a CONUNDRUM: MIT had the courses he wanted, but Harvard and Yale offered him full sports scholarships.*

convalescence *(con-vah-LESS-sense), noun*
The time you spend recovering from—and getting back to full health—after an illness, during which the patient usually rests while being taken care of by others.

> **"CONVALESCENCE** is the part that makes the illness worthwhile."
> **– George Bernard Shaw, Irish playwright**

convivial *(kuhn-VIV-ee-ull), adjective*
Fond of feasting, drinking, and companionship.
> *"One does not leave a CONVIVIAL party before closing time." – Winston Churchill, British statesman and orator*

coquette *(ko-KET), noun*
A woman who dresses promiscuously or flirts excessively to make men think she is sexually available when in fact she has no intention of sleeping with them.
> *Marla doesn't intend to play the COQUETTE at society balls, but her alluring looks attract other debutantes' dates constantly.*

countenance *(KOUN-tn-unts), noun*
A facial expression, either deliberate or unconscious, conveying the person's mood, thoughts, or emotions.
> *"We romped until the pans / Slid from the kitchen shelf; / My mother's COUNTENANCE / Could not unfrown itself." – Theodore Roethke, American poet*

coup *(koo), noun*
When a person already in a position of power forcibly seizes control.
> *Sophia took control of her father's company while he was in the hospital, an act the investors considered a bit of a COUP.*

couture *(kuh-TOUR), noun*
Clothing in the latest and most popular styles created by in-vogue fashion designers.
> *If Alyssia does not have the latest COUTURE prior to its debut on Paris runways, she will not deign to consider wearing it.*

cull *(KULL), verb*
To gather, amass, or collect.
> *Consumer behavior data was CULLED from online surveys and focus groups.*

cynosure *(SIN-uh-sure), noun*
A center of attention or attraction.
> *"This lighthouse was the CYNOSURE of all eyes." – Henry David Thoreau, American author and transcendentalist*

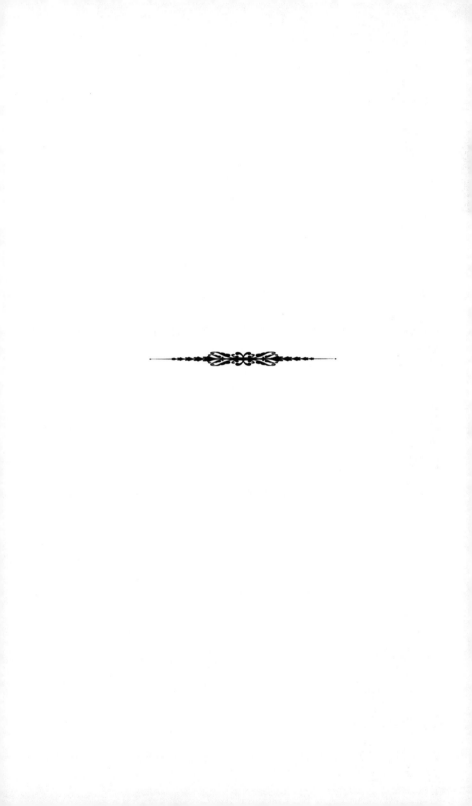

"Everything we shut our eyes to, everything we run away from, everything we deny, DENIGRATE or despise, serves to defeat us in the end."

———

Henry Miller, American author and painter

D

dalliance *(DAL-ee-anss), noun*
A brief, casual flirtation with or interest in someone or something; the act of tarrying rather than proceeding swiftly and deliberately.
> *Her DALLIANCE with the pool boy made her husband angry and jealous.*

D

dauntless *(DAWNT-liss), adjective*
Fearless, intrepid, and bold.

> "For Thought has a pair of **DAUNTLESS** wings." – *Robert Frost, American poet*

debauchery *(deh-BOW-chair-ee), noun*
Frequent indulgence in sensual pleasures.
> *"The geniuses, the mad dreamers, those who speak of DEBAUCHERY in the spirit, they are the condemned of our times." – Harlan Ellison, American author*

debilitate *(dih-BILL-uh-tayt), verb*
To make weak or feeble.
> *Several hours on the polo fields are enough to DEBILITATE even the most robust player.*

decimate *(DESS-ih-mate), verb*
To reduce something greatly, to the point of wiping it out.
> *"Every doctor will allow a colleague to DECIMATE a whole countryside sooner than violate the bond of professional etiquette by giving him away." – George Bernard Shaw, Irish playwright*

déclassé *(day-klass-AY), adjective*
Of a fallen social position or inferior status.
> *Jean thought her imitation designer bag looked exactly like the real thing, but the other girls in her exclusive private school quickly ridiculed Jean—and her bag—for being DÉCLASSÉ.*

decorous *(DEH-kore-us), adjective*
Behaving in a manner acceptable to polite society; having good taste and good manners.
> *"Another week with these DECOROUS drones and I'll jump out the window," the young girl complained to her mother of her fellow debutantes.*

de facto *(dee-FAK-toe), adjective*
Existing in fact.
> *Although we eschew titles, Sasha clearly is the DE FACTO head of our arts-patronage club.*

D

deflation *(dee-FLAY-shun), noun*
A weakened economy in which prices fall because of a decline in consumer spending.
> *We were pleased to learn that DEFLATION has not harmed sales at Wempe's on Fifth Avenue, our favorite purveyor of watches.*

defunct *(dih-FUNKT), adjective*
An institution, object, etc., that has ceased to exist.
> *"Practical men, who believe themselves to be quite exempt from any intellectual influence, are usually the slaves of some DEFUNCT economist."*
> *– John Maynard Keynes, British economist*

deification *(DEE-if-ih-kay-shin), noun*
The process of making someone or something into—and worshipping them as—a god.

"Poetry is the **DEIFICATION** of reality." *– Edith Sitwell, British poet*

deleterious *(dell-ih-TEAR-ee-us), adjective*
Harmful; damaging.
> *Smoking has been proven to have a DELETERIOUS effect on one's health.*

delineate *(dih-LINN-ee-ate), verb*
To use words to outline or describe with precision an object or person.
> *With efficiency, Prescott DELINEATED plans for the new wing of his family's Connecticut beach house.*

demagogue *(DEM-ah-gog), noun*
A politician who owes his popularity largely to pandering to popular opinion and catering to the wishes of his constituency.
> *"A DEMAGOGUE is a person with whom we disagree as to which gang should mismanage the country." – Don Marquis, American journalist and humorist*

demiurge *(DEM-ee-urj), noun*
A powerful creative force or a creative personality.
> *After trying a few different professions, Jackson realized that his ability with artifice, combined with his family connections, would make him a marketing DEMIURGE.*

demotic *(dih-MAH-tik), adjective*
Language used by ordinary people.
> *Eileen always avoids the DEMOTIC because she does not want to be mistaken for someone from the middle class.*

demur *(di-MURR), verb*
To make an objection on the grounds of scruples.
> *"Assent, and you are sane; / DEMUR,—you're straightway dangerous, / And handled with a chain." – Emily Dickinson, American poet*

denigrate *(DEN-ih-grayt), adjective*
Insulting; put down; demean; belittle.
> *"Everything we shut our eyes to, everything we run away from, everything we deny, DENIGRATE or despise, serves to defeat us in the end." – Henry Miller, American author and painter*

dénouement *(day-new-MAH), noun*
The conclusion of a complex series of events.
> *Marjorie was disappointed with the opera because she felt its DÉNOUEMENT left too many loose ends.*

deprecate *(DEPP-rih-kate), verb*
To express severe disapproval of another's actions.

> "Those who profess to favor freedom and yet **DEPRECATE** agitation, are men who want crops without plowing up the ground." – *Frederick Douglass, American abolitionist and orator*

de rigueur *(duh-rih-GUR), adjective*
Conforming to current standards of behavior, fashion, style, and etiquette.
> *A two-carat diamond engagement ring that cost a young man a year's salary was DE RIGUEUR for proposing to a girl in the 1950s.*

derivative *(deh-RIV-uh-tiv), adjective*
Copied or adapted from others.
> *"Only at his maximum does an individual surpass all his DERIVATIVE elements, and become purely himself." – D. H. Lawrence, British author*

descant *(des-KANT), verb*
To talk freely and without inhibition.
> *Eloise is always more than willing to DESCANT concerning her past liaisons.*

D

descry *(dih-SCRY), verb*
To make a discovery through careful examination.
> *With barely more than a casual glance, Amanda was able to DESCRY that the handbag was a knockoff.*

desideratum *(deh-sih-deh-RAH-tum), noun*
Something that one covets or desires.
> *Ever since she was an adolescent, Evangeline's DESIDERATUM has been a first edition of Virginia Woolf's first novel,* The Voyage Out.

desultory *(dee-SULL-ter-ee), adjective*
Acting without plan or purpose; activity that seems random or haphazard.

> "Find time still to be learning somewhat good, and give up being **DESULTORY**." *– Marcus Aurelius, Roman Emperor*

deus ex machina *(DAY-oos-eks-ma-KEEN-uh), noun*
An unexpected and fortunate event solving a problem or saving someone from disaster; a stroke of good luck.
> *The author used a DEUS EX MACHINA to work his way out of the mess he got the characters in toward the end of the novel.*

diaphanous *(die-APH-uh-nuss), adjective*
Fine and sheer; or, insubstantial and vague.
> *"To behold the day-break! / The little light fades the immense and DIAPHANOUS shadows, / The air tastes good to my palate." – Walt Whitman, American poet and humanist*

diatribe *(DIE-uh-tribe), noun*
A speech railing against injustice; a vehement denunciation.
The editorial was a mean-spirited DIATRIBE against school vouchers written to prevent children from other towns from being sent by bus to Centerville High School.

D

dichotomy *(die-KOT-uh-me), noun*
Division into two parts, especially into two seemingly contradictory parts.
A DICHOTOMY between good and evil is present in every human heart.

didactic *(dye-DAK-tik), adjective*
Designed, made, or tailored for purposes of education, self-improvement, or ethical betterment.
"The essential function of art is moral . . . but a passionate, implicit morality, not DIDACTIC." – D. H. Lawrence, British author

diffident *(DIFF-ih-dent), adjective*
To be uncertain or unsure about a making a decision or taking an action; to lack confidence and boldness.
If you feel DIFFIDENT about driving a Rolls Royce, you can always buy a Bentley.

dilettante *(DILL-ih-tont), noun*
A person who studies a subject in a casual fashion, learning the topic for the fun of it rather than to apply it to solve real problems.
Joseph Priestly could be considered a DILETTANTE, and yet his work led to the discovery of oxygen.

disabuse *(diss-uh-BYOOZ), verb*
To free oneself or someone else from an incorrect assumption or belief.
We had to DISABUSE Lorraine from her belief that her family connections would immediately make her a member of our group.

discomfit *(diss-KUM-fit), verb*
To embarrass someone to the point where they become uncomfortable.
Maggie's public mispronunciation of the designer's name at the charity benefit DISCOMFITED her mother.

discursive *(dis-KER-siv), adjective*
A manner or style of lecturing in which the speaker jumps back and forth between many topics.

Paul's DISCURSIVE lectures on American history jumped from century to century, yet it all came together in an understandable and fresh fashion.

disenfranchise *(dis-en-FRAN-chyz), verb*
To deny someone a right or privilege; to make someone feel rejected and apart.

D

"Some states specify felonies that condemn the citizen to DISENFRAN-CHISEMENT for life." – Andrew Hacker, American political scientist

dishabille *(dis-uh-BEE-uhl), noun*
Casual dress, or a casual manner.

Jensen is such a stickler for proper attire he feels he is in a state of DISHA-BILLE if he leaves the house without an ascot.

disparage *(dih-SPAIR-ihj), verb*
To bring reproach or discredit upon through one's words or actions.

"Man's constant need to DISPARAGE woman, to humble her, to deny her equal rights, and to belittle her achievements—all are expressions of his innate envy and fear." – Elizabeth Gould Davis, American feminist and author

disparate *(dis-PAHR-at), adjective*
Describes two or more things that differ greatly from one another and cannot be logically reconciled.

"As if, as if, as if the DISPARATE halves / Of things were waiting in a betrothal known / To none." – Wallace Stevens, American modernist poet

disport *(dih-SPOHRT), noun*
A diversion or amusement; can also be used as a verb, meaning to amuse oneself.

Felicia has turned the act of arguing with the proprietors of her favorite boutiques into a DISPORT.

disseminate *(diss-SEM-in-ate), verb*
To distribute something so as to make it available to a large population or area.

The Internet is rapidly replacing newspapers as the primary medium for the DISSEMINATION of news.

dissimulate *(diss-IHM-you-late), verb*
To hide one's feelings from another by using untruths.

"To know how to DISSIMULATE is the knowledge of kings." – Cardinal Richelieu, French clergyman, noble, and statesman

diurnal *(die-URN-al), adjective*
Taking place or being active during daylight hours.
> *The house staff knows not even to approach Nora's bedroom door before twilight because she totally rejects a DIURNAL lifestyle.*

dogmatic *(DAWG-matt-ick), adjective*
A person who adheres rigidly to principles, rules, and beliefs, even when there is ample evidence that doing so may not be the best course of action.
> *Leroy is DOGMATIC in his assertion that the Maserati Gran Turismo is superior to the Mercedes-Benz SLR McLaren.*

douceur *(doo-SIR), noun*
A bribe or a conciliatory gift.
> *After Francine's father refused to buy her another polo pony, he offered her the DOUCEUR of a weekend at an exclusive spa.*

doyen/doyenne *(doy-EN), noun*
A man or woman who is the senior member of a group, based on rank, age, experience, etc.
> *Though she is the youngest member of our group, Brittany is our DOYENNE, based on her extensive family connections.*

Draconian *(drah-KONE-ee-an), adjective*
Strict; mean-spirited; excessively harsh; cruel; punishment or restriction meant to cause misery to those receiving it.
> *Ophelia was distraught over the DRACONIAN way that her father forced her to stay with her chaperone throughout their vacation on the Greek Isles.*

duffer *(DUFF-uhr), noun*
An incompetent or ineffectual person.
> *Maxwell can't help being a DUFFER. After all, his family has only been wealthy for two generations.*

dyslogistic *(diz-luh-JISS-tick), adjective*
Showing disapproval or censure.
> *We gave Elizabeth DYSLOGISTIC glances when she told us she had decided to stop shopping at Cartier.*

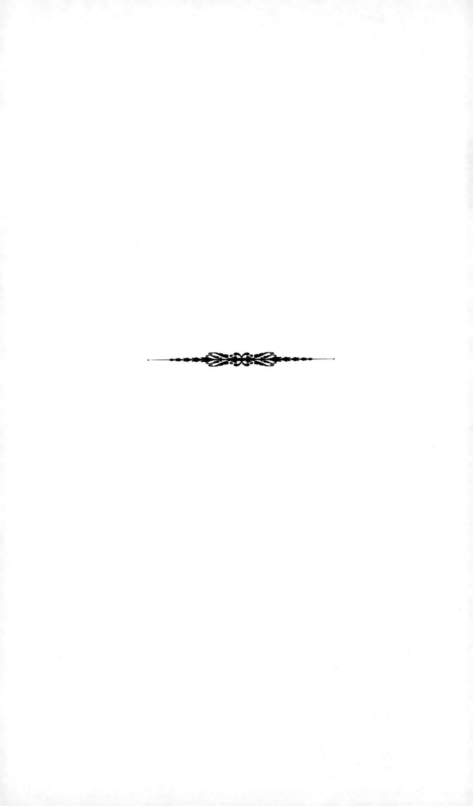

"There is no man, however wise, who has not at some period of his youth said things, or lived in a way the consciousness of which is so unpleasant to him in later life that he would gladly, if he could, EXPUNGE it from his memory."

———

Marcel Proust, French novelist, essayist, and critic

E

earmark *(EER-mark), verb*
To set aside money to be used for a specific purpose.
> *Milly's earnings from her job were EARMARKED for her son's college tuition.*

E

ebullient *(EB-you-lent), adjective*
Feeling joy and positive emotions at an extreme level; the state of being wildly enthusiastic about something.
> *Lorne was EBULLIENT when he found that his mother had given the college enough money to overturn his rejection.*

echelon *(ESH-uh-lonn), noun*
A level of command or authority.
> *Family connections helped Michael ascend quickly to the upper ECHELON of his brokerage firm.*

éclat *(ay-KLAH), noun*
Great public acclaim; or, great public notoriety.
> *Although they are the height of Paris fashion, Martina's five-inch heels earned her much ÉCLAT in the society pages.*

edacious *(ih-DAY-shuss), adjective*
Greedy, eager, and consumed with consumption.
> *It's not fair to label Rosella EDACIOUS because she only wants the same luxury items the rest of us desire.*

educe *(ee-DYOOCE), verb*
To come to a conclusion or solve a problem through reasoning based on thoughtful consideration of the facts.
> *After Roger's family purchased a Mercedes C class, rather than its usual Mercedes E class, we EDUCED the Wallertons were enduring financial difficulties.*

efface *(ih-FAYSS), verb*
To erase, obliterate, make inconspicuous.

> "It is also true that one can write nothing readable unless one constantly struggles to **EFFACE** one's own personality. Good prose is like a windowpane." – *George Orwell, British author*

effervescent *(ef-ur-VES-ent), adjective*
Bubbly; upbeat; cheerful; possessing a positive attitude and joyful personality.
> *After getting the acceptance letter from Cornell, Sabrina was positively EFFERVESCENT and celebrated with a trip to Neiman Marcus.*

E

effete *(eh-FEET), adjective*
Decadent and lacking in vigor due to decadence or self-indulgence.
> *The Eddingtons donated one of their serving sets to charity, so only the truly EFFETE would deign to label the family as snobs.*

efficacious *(eff-ih-KAY-shuss), adjective*
Capable of having a desired effect.
> *"Example is always more EFFICACIOUS than precept." – Samuel Johnson, British moralist and poet*

efflorescent *(ef-luh-RES-uhnt), adjective*
Describes something that has reached the final stage of its development or is at the peak of perfection.
> *Thomas is convinced that the Bugati Veyron Fbg represents the EFFLORESCENT automobile.*

effrontery *(eh-FRON-ter-ee), noun*
To have offended someone through inappropriate or aggressive behavior or audacious requests; audacity.
> *After doing a terrible job on the project, he had the EFFRONTERY to ask me, "Can I do extra credit?"*

effulgent *(ih-FULL-junt), adjective*
Shining brightly; glowing; radiant.
> *The lightning storm made the evening sky positively EFFULGENT.*

effusive *(eh-FEW-siv), adjective*
Profuse and overflowing, without reservation.
> *In an effort to butter up the senator, the lobbyist was transparently EFFUSIVE in his praise of the new bill.*

egalitarian *(ih-gal-uh-TARE-ee-uhn), adjective*
To be fair and balanced in the extreme; to act in the belief that all men are created equal and should be treated so.
> *"Chinks in America's EGALITARIAN armor are not hard to find. Democracy is the fig leaf of elitism." – Florence King, American author*

egregious *(E-GREE-jus), adjective*
A serious mistake or offense, often with dire consequences.
Pauline made the EGREGIOUS mistake of asking the price of a piece of jewelry that caught her eye, rather than simply asking to purchase the necklace.

E

eidetic *(aye-DETT-ick), adjective*
Of visual imagery that is nearly photographic in detail.
We were displeased with the Howlands' recent art purchase because the so-called artist harkens back to the tired old school of EIDETIC representation.

eidolon *(eye-DOH-luhn), noun*
A phantom or apparition; or, the image of an ideal.

"By a route obscure and lonely, / Haunted by ill angels only, / Where an **EIDOLON**, named Night, / On a black throne reigns upright." – *Edgar Allan Poe, American author and poet*

élan, *(ey-LAN), noun*
Enthusiasm, energy, flair, zest.
Bryanna reacted with ÉLAN when she was tapped to be part of a feature for Elite Travel Magazine.

elegy *(EL-eh-gee), noun*
A lament for the dead.
"Modern ELEGIES tend to be unconvincing because the poet so clearly believes in the immortality that an ELEGY traditionally claims for its subject." – Edward Mendelson, Professor of English and Comparative Literature at Colombia University

elide *(ee-LIDE), verb*
To leave out a sound or syllable when speaking; to eliminate the distinctive barrier separating levels.
When Catherine ELIDES the "g's" at the end of certain words, she betrays her Southern origins.

elocution *(el-oh-CUE-shun), noun*
The ability to deliver a public speech in a clear and persuasive manner.
He's a brilliant man, but he needs to work on his ELOCUTION.

elucidate *(ee-LOO-sih-date), verb*
To lecture, explain, or pontificate about a subject in great detail so as to make it exceeding clear.
> *"It [was] the mission of the twentieth century to ELUCIDATE the irrational." – Maurice Merleau -Ponty, French philosopher*

E

elucubrate *(ih-LOO-kyoo-brait), verb*
To produce a written work through lengthy, intensive effort.
> *Thanks to a few hundred bucks passed along to a classmate, Miles did not have to ELUCUBRATE his term paper and could, instead, attend parties with us.*

emend *(ih-MEND), verb*
To correct or remove faults, as from a text.
> *Blanche EMENDED her holiday wish list, removing the Ferrari watch and replacing it with a Versace dinner plate.*

empressement *(ahn-press-MAH), noun*
A display of effusive cordiality.
> *Those at the party who belonged to the nouveau riche set were easy to recognize, due to their constant and distasteful EMPRESSEMENT.*

empyreal *(em-PEER-ee-uhl), adjective*
Elevated and sublime; or, of the sky
> *The beautiful three-carat sapphire her fiancé gave her shone with an EMPYREAL, almost celestial, light.*

encipher *(en-SY-fur), verb*
To scramble or convert data into a secret code, prior to transmission, thereby making it impossible for unauthorized users to understand or decipher.
> *Mathematicians were employed by the Army to crack ENCIPHERED messages during the war.*

encomium *(en-KO-me-um), noun*
Effusive praise given in a public forum.
> *The CEO's ENCOMIUM at Phil's retirement dinner caused his eyes to mist over.*

endemic *(en-DEM-ik), adjective*
A widespread condition or characteristic found in a certain region, area, or group.
> *Affluence and influence seem to be just ENDEMIC to our group.*

enervate *(EN-er-vayt), transitive verb*
To rob a person, organization, place, or thing of its energy, strength, and vitality.
> *Greenhouse gases ENERVATE the protective ozone layer surrounding the Earth.*

E

enigmatic *(en-ig-MATT-ik), adjective*
Mysterious, puzzling, and difficult to figure out.
> *"The interest in life does not lie in what people do, nor even in their relations to each other, but largely in the power to communicate with a third party, antagonistic, ENIGMATIC, yet perhaps persuadable, which one may call life in general." – Virginia Woolf, British essayist and novelist*

enjoin *(ehn-JOYN), verb*
To direct or order someone to do something.
> *After purchasing one too many Bentleys, Alex's father ENJOINED him to be more frugal.*

enmity *(EN-mih-tee), noun*
Mutual dislike, animosity, hatred, antagonism, or disagreement between two groups or parties.
> *Was the ENMITY between Muhammad Ali and Joe Frasier an act, genuine, or a combination of both?*

ennui *(on-WEE), noun*
Apathy and lack of energy caused by boredom and disinterest.
> *"And he spoke of ENNUI, of jaded appetites, of nights and days aboard a moonstone vessel as large as a city." – Harlan Ellison, American author*

ensconce *(en-SKONTS), verb*
To settle oneself warmly or snugly; or, to hide something in a secure place.
> *Julia ENSCONSED herself in a leather chair in the family's library and perused recent catalogues.*

entropy *(EN-troh-pee), noun*
The tendency of any system to run down and revert to total chaos.

> "Just as the constant increase of **ENTROPY** is the basic law of the universe, so it is the basic law of life to be ever more highly structured and to struggle against **ENTROPY**." – *Václav Havel, Czech playwright, writer, and politician*

enumerate *(eh-NOO-muh-rate), verb*
To list or to count off individually, one by one.
> *"One might ENUMERATE the items of high civilization, as it exists in other countries, which are absent from the texture of American life, until it should become a wonder to know what was left." – Henry James, American-born British author*

enunciate *(ee-NUN-see-ate), verb*
To pronounce words carefully and clearly; to speak in a manner that makes you easily understood.
> *No one will listen to him until he stops mumbling and learns to ENUNCIATE.*

envisage *(en-VIZ-ij), verb*
To envision, imagine, or create a mental picture.
> *"I don't ENVISAGE collectivism. There is no such animal, it is always individualism." – Gertrude Stein, American author*

ephemeral *(eh-FEM-er-uhl), adjective*
Describes a short-lived condition, temporary event, or fleeting moment.

> "There remain some truths too **EPHEMERAL** to be captured in the cold pages of a court transcript." – **Irving Kaufman, Chief Judge, United States Court of Appeals**

epicurean *(eh-pih-CURE-ee-an), noun*
Devoted to the enjoyment of good food and comfort.
> *Mother's Thanksgiving meal at the Cape Cod compound was an annual EPICUREAN delight.*

epigraph *(EH-pih-graf), noun*
A short quotation or saying at the beginning of a book or book chapter, or a brief inscription on a coin, statue, or building.
> *"Benfey begins his book with a curious EPIGRAPH from John Ruskin." – Joyce Carol Oates, American author*

epiphany *(eh-PIH-fan-see), noun*
A sudden, unexpected insight that seems to come from nowhere and throws great illumination on a subject previously not well understood.
> *One day Marcus had an EPIPHANY and realized that, to find true happiness, he should become a philanthropist.*

epistolary *(eh-PISS-toe-lar-ee), adjective*
Having to do with writing or letters or other literary works.
> *Madeline continues the EPISTOLARY tradition by eschewing e-mail, opting for fine parchment and her great-grandfather's diamond-encrusted quill pen for her correspondence.*

E

eponymous *(eh-PON-eh-muss), adjective*
To be named after something, such as a child being named after his grandfather or the mythical Romulus giving his name to Rome.
> *Josephine spends as much time as possible sailing in her EPONYMOUS yacht.*

equable *(ECK-wuh-bull), adjective*
Unvarying, steady, and free from extremes.
> *"He spake of love, such love as spirits feel / In worlds whose course is EQUABLE and pure." – William Wordsworth, British Romantic poet*

equanimity *(ee-kwa-NIM-ih-tee), noun*
The ability to keep one's cool during times of stress, conflict, or trouble.
> *When his mother locked her keys in the car, her young son responded with surprising EQUANIMITY.*

equivocate *(ee-KWIV-uh-kate), verb*
To change one's mind or be unable to stick with a decision or resolution; to vacillate in one's opinion or position.
> *The candidate seemed to EQUIVOCATE on the energy crisis with each speech he made.*

ersatz *(Er-ZATS), adjective*
A phony, a fake, a counterfeit, an inferior copy, a pale imitation of an original.
> *Before his sentencing and jail term, the artist made an impressive living selling ERSATZ Rembrandt paintings.*

erudite *(AIR-yoo-dyte), adjective*
Sophisticated; well educated; deeply learned; knowledgeable; scholarly.
> *Beneath his ERUDITE image, Dr. John Brinkley was a money-grubbing con man.*

esoteric *(es-oh-TER-ik), adjective*
Something known or appreciated by an elite few who have the taste, sophistication, and education to understand its merits.

"My ESOTERIC doctrine, is that if you entertain any doubt, it is safest to take the unpopular side in the first instance." – William Lamb Melbourne, British prime minister

ethereal *(eh-THEER-ee-uhl), adjective*
Light and airy; possessing a heavenly or celestial quality.
"ETHEREAL, their mauve / almost a transparent gray, / their dark veins / bruise-blue." – Denise Levertov, British-born American poet

E

ethos *(EE-thos), noun*
The core principles or beliefs of a religion, culture, or community.
Even the eating of cheese violates the ETHOS of the vegan culture.

etiolate *(EE-tee-uh-late), verb*
To cause something to become weak and appear sickly.
Over time, Brad's excesses—and his refusal to see a plastic surgeon—increasingly ETIOLATED his once-handsome appearance.

euphemism *(YOU-feh-miz-im), noun*
A synonym that is less offensive than the word it is used to replace.
"The doctor told me I'm big boned," said Chuck defensively. "That's just a EUPHEMISM for fat," his brother said meanly.

euphuism *(YOU-few-iz-im), noun*
A phrase, sentence, or thought expressed in an ornate, flowery, overly elaborate style of writing, often making the exact meaning difficult to discern.
Felicia's words are full of EUPHUISM, particularly when describing the architecture of her family's various houses.

euphony *(YOU-fone-ee), noun*
The habit of changing the pronunciation of words or the wording of phrases so they are pleasing to the ear and roll off the tongue with greater ease.
In finishing school, Alsace learned the art of EUPHONY, and she has parlayed that into a hobby of earning roles in television commercials.

eustasy *(YEW-stah-see), noun*
A change in sea level caused by melting of ice, movement of ocean floors, or major deposits of sediment.
Global warming is already triggering EUSTASY with the melting of the polar ice caps.

evanescent *(ev-eh-NESS-ent), adjective*
Having the qualities of a mist or vapor, capable of vanishing seemingly into thin air.
> *"Nobody thinks it's silly to invest two hours' work in two minutes' enjoyment; but if cooking is EVANESCENT, well, so is the ballet." – Julia Child, American cook, author, and television personality*

evince *(ee-VINCE), verb*
To reveal or indicate the presence of a particular feeling or condition.
> *The blocky lines of Van Gogh's paintings EVINCE a feeling of depression and madness.*

exacerbate *(egg-ZASS-err-bayt), verb*
To take action that makes a situation worse or aggravates it further.
> *The problem with the mission was further EXACERBATED when the outer tiles ripped away from the space shuttle.*

excoriate *(eggs-KORE-ee-ate), verb*
To criticize; to attempt to censure or punish.
> *We EXCORIATED Melanie for inviting people with no family connections to her birthday party.*

exculpate *(EKS-kull-payte), verb*
To prove the innocence of someone suspected of being guilty, or free someone from an obligation or burden.
> *Gerald Ford's pardon EXCULPATED Richard Nixon legally, but history consigned him to the role of a disgraced president forever.*

execrate *(EGGS-eh-krayt), verb*
To loath; to subject to scorn and derision.
> *We EXECRATED William for weeks due to his casual rejection of an invitation to join Yale's Skull and Bones.*

exemplar *(eggs-EM-plar), noun*
A role model, a shining example of a desired state, status, or behavior.
> *"The system—the American one, at least—is a vast and noble experiment. It has been polestar and EXAMPLAR for other nations." – Phyllis McGinley, American poet*

exhort *(ig-ZORT), verb*
To urge or advise earnestly.
> *"The function of the moralist is not to EXHORT men to be good but to elucidate what the good is." – Walter Lippman, American journalist*

exigency *(EKS-ih-jen-see), noun*
A condition or problem of some urgency, such that when it arises, it requires an immediate effort to alleviate or solve it.

> "We should never despair, our Situation before has been unpromising and has changed for the better, so I trust, it will again. If new difficulties arise, we must only put forth New Exertions and proportion our Efforts to the **EXIGENCY** of the times." – *George Washington*

E

existential *(eggs-ih-STEN-shul), adjective*
Refers to ideas, beliefs, and philosophies that support the belief in free will and the freedom of the individual.

> *"No phallic hero, no matter what he does to himself or to another to prove his courage, ever matches the solitary, EXISTENTIAL courage of the woman who gives birth." – Andrea Dworkin, American radical feminist and author*

expropriate *(eks-PRO-pree-ate), verb*
To seize property or wealth from its owner for the public's use or benefit, as when the state takes someone's home under eminent domain to build a road through it.

> *The Bradfords are still reeling from the fact that the state EXPROPRIATED a portion of their formal gardens for a new highway.*

expurgate *(EKS-per-gate), transitive verb*
To purge sexually inappropriate, disgusting, or otherwise undesirable material prior to presentation.

> *For her parents' benefit, Marina EXPURGATED stories related to the weekend she spent slumming in Greenwich Village.*

extemporaneous *(eks-tem-POOR-ayne-ee-us), adjective*
Off the cuff; done without preparation.

> *My ability to speak EXTEMPORANEOUSLY makes me very comfortable speaking in front of a group that asks a lot of questions.*

extol *(eks-TOLE), verb*
To praise with great enthusiasm.

> *Iris has not ceased to EXTOL the virtues of her new Romain Jerome Day & Night Watch.*

expunge *(eks-PUNJ), verb*

To rid oneself of an annoyance; to cast out; to get rid of; to forcibly eject.

> *"There is no man, however wise, who has not at some period of his youth said things, or lived in a way the consciousness of which is so unpleasant to him in later life that he would gladly, if he could, EXPUNGE it from his memory." – Marcel Proust, French novelist, essayist, and critic*

extrapolate *(eks-TRAP-oh-late), verb*

To infer, by taking known information into account.

> *The tasteful four-carat diamond on her finger allowed us to EXTRAPO-LATE that Portia had accepted James's proposal.*

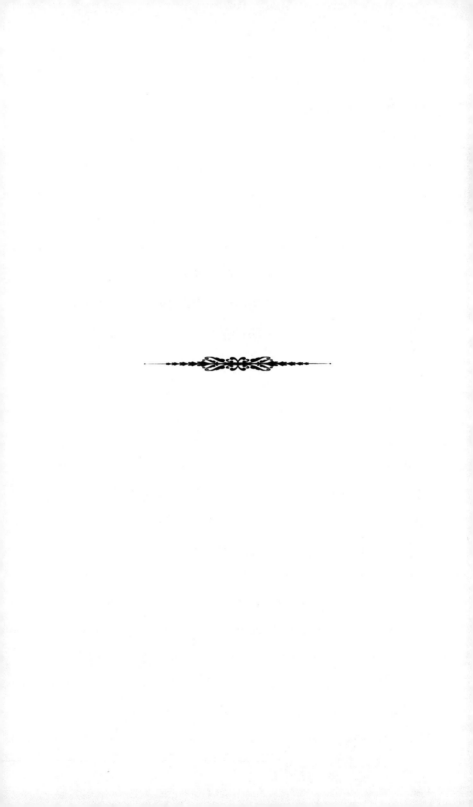

"Never lose sight of the fact that all human FELICITY lies in man's imagination, and that he cannot think to attain it unless he heeds all his caprices."

———

Marquis de Sade, French aristocrat and revolutionary

façade *(fah-SAHD), noun*
The front of a building; a deceptive appearance masking a thing's true nature.

> "A good man often appears gauche simply because he does not take advantage of the myriad mean little chances of making himself look stylish. Preferring truth to form, he is not constantly at work upon the **FAÇADE** of his appearance." – *Iris Murdoch, Irish writer and philosopher*

facetious *(fuh-SEE-shus), adjective*
Comments made specifically to get a laugh out of those around you; something said in jest; sarcastic.
> *"Boarding school manners and attitudes—stoic denial, FACETIOUS irony—are still deeply entrenched in the character of the country." – Jonathan Raban, British travel writer and novelist*

facile *(FASS-ill), adjective*
Accomplished easily and with little effort.

> "The hunger for **FACILE** wisdom is the root of all false philosophy." - *George Santayana, Spanish-born American author and philosopher*

faction *(FAK-shin), noun*
A small dissenting group within a larger one.
> *"I will keep where there is wit stirring, and leave the FACTION of fools." – William Shakespeare*

factitious *(fack-TISH-uss), adjective*
Contrived; fabricated.
> *At first, we thought the rumor FACTITIOUS, but then we learned that couture-producer Hermes does, in fact, plan to design and market a helicopter.*

fallacious *(fuh-LAY-shus), adjective*
An idea or conclusion based on one or more false assumptions.
> *Since my online subscriber list is double opt-in, accusing me of being a spammer is a wholly FALLACIOUS assumption.*

fallible *(FAL-ih-bull), adjective*
Capable of screwing up, making errors, or being wrong.
At a fairly young age children realize their parents are eminently FALLIBLE.

farcical *(FAR-sih-kuhl), adjective*
Ludicrous, absurd, or laughably inept.
"To conjure up such ridiculous questions, the answers to which we all know or should know are in the negative, is to build up a whimsical and FARCICAL straw man which is not only grim but Grimm." – Tom C. Clark, Supreme Court Justice

farouche *(fah-ROSH), adjective*
To become sullen, shy, or withdrawn in the presence of company.
His FAROUCHE demeanor gave people the impression that he didn't like them, when in fact, he was merely an introvert.

fastidious *(fah-STID-ee-us), adjective*
To be particular about things, particularly good housekeeping and personal hygiene; to place great importance on even the smallest of details.

"A **FASTIDIOUS** person in the throes of love is a rich source of mirth."
– Martha Duffy, Arts editor, Time *magazine*

fatuous *(FACH-oo-us), adjective*
Trivial, silly, absurd, unimportant, pointless.
"I'm sick of pretending that some FATUOUS male's self-important pronouncements are the objects of my undivided attention." – Germaine Greer, Australian writer and scholar

Faustian *(FOW-stee-in), adjective*
Evil; malicious; dark and brooding with malevolent intent; demonic; satanic; having sold one's soul to the devil—metaphorically or literally—in exchange for wealth and power.
In the movie The End of Days *a group of police officers make a FAUSTIAN bargain with Satan himself.*

faux *(FOH), adjective*
Fake; phony; artificial.
She wore a cheap second-hand dress and a FAUX pearl necklace made out of white beads.

faux pas *(FOH pah), noun*
A serious breach of social protocol or etiquette.
> *Looking a Japanese business customer directly in the eye during conversation is considered an egregious FAUX PAS not easily forgiven.*

fealty *(FEE-ul-tea), noun*
A sense of obligation or loyalty, usually existing because one person feels beholden to another.
> *The only reason that Bryson pledged FEALTY to David is because David's social connections helped Bryson get a job on Wall Street.*

feckless *(FEK-less), adjective*
Possessing an air of casual indifference; lacking definitiveness of purpose.
> *Some accuse us of being FECKLESS, but they have no idea how difficult it is to live a wealth-infused lifestyle.*

fecundity *(Fe-KUN-di-tee), noun*
A person, organization, resource, or activity that is exceptionally productive, creative, fertile, or fruitful.
> *"Blistering heat suddenly took the place of Carboniferous moisture and FECUNDITY." – Simon Winchester, British author and journalist*

felicitous *(fih-LISS-ih-tuss), adjective*
Appropriate and well suited for a particular occasion.
> *"O to be a dragon / a symbol of the power of Heaven—of silkworm / size or immense; at times invisible. FELICITOUS phenomenon!" – Marianne Moore, Modernist American poet and writer*

felicity *(fih-LISS-ih-tee), noun*
A state of blissful happiness.
> *"Never lose sight of the fact that all human FELICITY lies in man's imagination, and that he cannot think to attain it unless he heeds all his caprices." - Marquis de Sade, French aristocrat and revolutionary*

fervent *(FUR-vuhnt), adjective*
Showing great enthusiasm and intensity of spirit.
> *Packing up the family's castoffs for myriad charities each December places Contessa in a FERVENT state.*

fiat *(FEE-aht), noun*
An authoritative decree or order.

Everyone interested in receiving a sizeable portion of his inheritance simply allows grandfather to rule the household by FIAT.

filibuster *(FILL-in-bus-ter), noun*
Making a prolonged speech or using other tactics to delay legislative actions or other important decisions.

The room breathed a collective sigh when the senator finally ended his eight-hour FILIBUSTER.

fillip *(FILL-uhp), noun*
Something that revives or arouses excitement.

"Faithful horoscope-watching, practiced daily, provides just the sort of small, but warm and infinitely reassuring FILLIP that gets matters off to a spirited start." – Shana Alexander, American author

flagitious *(fluh-JISH-uss), adjective*
Shamefully wicked or particularly heinous.

Now that the paparazzi hangs on her every move, Natasha goes out of her way to engage in FLAGITIOUS behavior.

flagrante delicto *(fluh-grahn-tay di-LIK-toh), noun*
In the act of committing an offense; most widely used today to describe a couple caught in the act of sexual intercourse.

"No cheating spouse, no teen with a wrecked family car, no mayor of Washington, DC, videotaped in FLAGRANTE DELICTO has ever come up with anything as farfetched as U.S. farm policy." – P. J. O'Rourke, American satirist

florid *(FLOOR-id), adjective*
Excessively ornate and showy, as prose.

"All men are really most attracted by the beauty of plain speech, and they even write in a **FLORID** style in imitation of this." – *Henry David Thoreau, American author and transcendentalist*

foible *(FOY-bull), noun*
A small flaw, weakness, or defect.

For all his flaws and FOIBLES, Richard Nixon was perhaps the most effective president on foreign policy in the twentieth century.

foment *(foe-MEHNT), verb*
To rouse or incite.

> "If perticuliar care and attention is not paid to the Laidies we are determined to **FOMENT** a Rebelion, and will not hold ourselves bound by any Laws in which we have no voice, or Representation." – *Abigail Adams, second First Lady of the United States*

forbear *(for-BEAR), verb*
To not do something; to do without.
> *The landlord decided to FORBEAR raising the rent until the repairs to the building had been completed.*

forestall *(for-STAWL), verb*
To thwart an action in advance; or, to buy up goods in order to increase their resale price.
> *Arthur's family thrives during financially insecure times because it always seems to FORESTALL exactly the right commodities.*

fortuitous *(for-TOO-ih-tuss), adjective*
A happy event taking place by accident or chance.
> *"The most FORTUITOUS event of my entire life was meeting my wife Eleanor." – Franklin Delano Roosevelt*

founder *(FOUN-der), verb*
To fail utterly or to become a complete wreck.
> *"Who would not rather FOUNDER in the fight / Than not have known the glory of the fray?" – Richard Hovey, American poet*

fractious *(FRACK-shuss), adjective*
Easily angered or irritable; quarrelsome; unruly.
> *"Sex is metaphysical for men, as it is not for women. Women have no problem to solve through sex. Physically and psychologically, they are serenely self-contained. They may choose to achieve, but they do not need it. They are not thrust into the beyond by their own FRACTIOUS bodies." – Camille Paglia, American author, feminist, and social critic*

frangible *(FRAN-juh-bull), adjective*
Easily breakable.

*The Worthington's staff knows to be excessively careful around the fami-
lies collection of FRANGIBLE Ming vases.*

frenetic *(fruh-NET-ick), adjective*
Frantic and frenzied.
> *"I love my work with a FRENETIC and perverse love, as an ascetic loves
> the hair shirt which scratches his belly." – Gustave Flaubert, French
> writer*

F

frippery *(FRIHP-uh-ree), noun*
Ostentatious or affected elegance.
> *The FRIPPERY of Lara's couture belied her nouveau riche origins.*

frisson *(FREE-son), noun*
A sudden strong feeling of excitement, conflict, or danger.
> *"Pregnant women! They had that weird FRISSON, an aura of magic
> that combined awkwardly with an earthy sense of duty." – Ruth Morgan,
> American novelist*

fruition *(froo-ISH-un), noun*
The completion of a task; the achievement of a goal as the result of significant and persistent effort.
> *John Nash, a mathematician whose life was featured in "A Beautiful
> Mind," received the Nobel Prize for the FRUITION of his work in game
> theory decades after he completed it.*

fulsome *(FULL-sum), adjective*
Describes words or actions that praise or flatter someone to an excessive
degree.
> *Katie's introduction of the keynote speaker was so FULSOME that he led
> his speech with a few self-effacing remarks.*

fungible *(FUHN-jih-bull), adjective*
Freely exchangeable for another of like nature; interchangeable.
> *Stella was incensed to find that not all Cartier watches are FUNGIBLE.*

furtive *(FUR-tiv), adjective*
Acting guilty of some misstep or possessing knowledge one would just as
soon keep secret.
> *"For a while the two stared at each other – Denison embarrassed, Selene
> almost FURTIVE." – Isaac Asimov, Russian-born American author and
> biochemist*

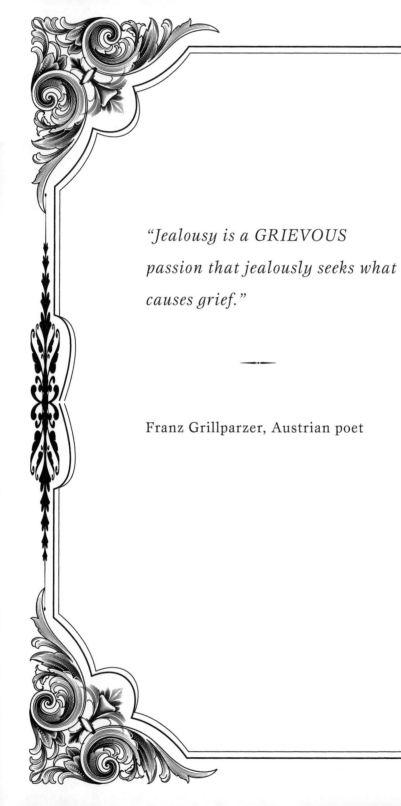

"Jealousy is a GRIEVOUS passion that jealously seeks what causes grief."

Franz Grillparzer, Austrian poet

gable *(GAY-bull), noun*
The triangular upper part of a wall at the end of a rigid roof.
The Sandersons could not resist purchasing a second Cape Cod home because they fell in love with the home's colorful GABLES.

gainsay *(GANE-say), verb*
To deny, dispute, or contradict.
Michael has made no attempt to GAINSAY the persistent rumors that his family's fortune rests solely on insider trading.

galivant *(GAL-ih-vant), verb*
To wander widely; to constantly travel to many different places, without an itinerary or plan; to freely go wherever and whenever the mood strikes you, and doing so frequently.
Some accuse us of GALIVANTING around the world, but cultural knowledge is de rigueur for cocktail conversation.

galleon *(GAL-ee-un), noun*
A Mediterranean sailing vessel used by explorers for ocean voyages.
The GALLEONS of the Spanish fleet sailed annually from Seville to Panama and Cartagena.

galvanize *(GAL-vuh-nyze), verb*
To propel someone or something into sudden activity.
The unveiling of new yachts quickly GALVANIZED the regatta.

gambit *(GAM-bit), noun*
A remark used to redirect a conversation; or a maneuver used to seek advantage.
"The catchphrase positively rejoices in being a formula, an accepted GAMBIT, a ready-made reaction." – John Gross, British literary critic

gambol *(GAM-bowl), verb*
To run, skip, or jump about in a playful or joyous fashion.
"We all have these places where shy humiliations GAMBOL on sunny afternoons." – W. H. Auden, Anglo-American poet

gamesome *(GAYM-suhm), adjective*
Playful and frolicsome.
"[Nature] is GAMESOME and good, / But of mutable mood,— / No dreary repeater now and again, / She will be all things to all men." – Ralph Waldo Emerson, American poet, essayist, and transcendentalist

gamine *(gah-MEEN), noun*
A girl with a boyish demeanor and mischievous nature who is somehow still appealing.

> *Her GAMINE behavior and looks only made her that much more attractive to teenage boys her age.*

gamut *(GAM-utt), noun*
The full spectrum of possibilities or choices.

> *The choice of places to eat near the mall ran the GAMUT from chain restaurants to five-star dining.*

garnish *(GAR-nihsh), verb*
A legal procedure for taking a portion of a person's wages, property, and assets to pay his debts.

> *If you do not pay your taxes within thirty days, the county reserves the right to GARNISH a portion of your wages until the back taxes are paid in full.*

garrulity *(gah-ROO-lih-tee), noun*
The habit of talking way too much.

> "The interview is an intimate conversation between journalist and politician wherein the journalist seeks to take advantage of the **GARRULITY** of the politician and the politician of the credulity of the journalist" – *Emory Klein, American journalist*

gauche *(GOHSH), adjective*
Sorely lacking in the social graces and good manners; crude behavior.

> *Rhett was under the impression that one needed only money to join the country club. However, his GAUCHE demeanor caused him to be denied membership.*

gazetteer *(gaz-ih-TEERr), noun*
A geographical index or dictionary of places organized by name.

> *The Rothschilds prefer their pilot simply head for the sun, rather than consult a GAZETTEER prior to short flights.*

gelid *(JELL-uhd), adjective*
extremely cold; icy.

> *The Vangelder's yacht sluiced easily through the GELID waters of the Cape.*

genome *(GEE-nome), noun*
The collection of chromosomes that makes an individual organism unique from all others except its clone or identical twin.

> *Blake has become convinced that the GENOMES of those among his most important social contacts have more commonalities than differences.*

genteel *(jehn-TEEL), adjective*
Well-bred and possessing a refined temperament.

> "[I am] a journalist in the field of etiquette. I try to find out what the most **GENTEEL** people regularly do, what traditions they have discarded, what compromises they have made." – *Amy Vanderbilt, American etiquette expert*

geopolitical *(gee-oh-poh-LIH-tih-kull), adjective*
Anything having to do with the politics affecting the relationships of two or more countries, especially when influenced by geographical factors.

> *GEOPOLITICAL instability in the Middle East is fueling rising crude oil prices.*

geostationary *(GEE-oh-STAY-shin-air-ee), adjective*
A satellite in orbit 22,300 miles above the Earth's surface so that the satellite is always directly over the same spot of ground.

> *Arthur C. Clark was the first to propose that three GEOSTATIONARY satellites orbiting Earth could provide a global communications network effectively covering every location on the planet.*

germane *(jehr-MANE), adjective*
Relevant, pertinent, and fitting.

> "*Quotes from Mao, Castro, and Che Guevara . . . are as GERMANE to our highly technological, computerized society as a stagecoach on a jet runway at Kennedy airport.*" – *Saul Alinksy, American activist*

germinal *(JUHRM-nuhl), adjective*
Related to the earliest stage of development.

> *Roland's foray into art-buying is in its GERMINAL phase.*

gestalt *(geh-STALT), noun*
A unified whole.

> "*Feminism is an entire world view or GESTALT, not just a laundry list of women's issues.*" – *Charlotte Bunch, American feminist*

gesticulate *(jes-TIH-cue-late), verb*
To use gestures when talking, especially when speaker is eager or excited to get his ideas across.
"Okay, the man in the yellow shirt," the seminar leader said, pointing to an audience member who was GESTICULATING wildly.

gimcrack *(JIHM-krack), noun*
A showy object of little or no value.
"Haul them off! Hide them! / The heart winces / For junk and GIM-CRACK, / for jerrybuilt things." – Richard Wilbur, American poet

glean *(GLEEN), verb*
To discover or learn slowly and deliberately.
Bentley GLEANED from the drop in Ferrari sales that a looming recession even had some of his social contacts feeling nervous.

globalization *(glow-bull-ih-ZAY-shin), noun*
The movement toward a true world economy with open and free trading across national borders.
"Proponents of GLOBALIZATION insist that, as trade and investment move across borders, economic efficiencies raise the standards of living on both sides of the exchange." – Arthur Goldwag, American author

globule *(GLAHB-yewl), noun*
A small globe or ball.
"In yourself is the law of all nature, and you know not yet how a GLOB-ULE of sap ascends." – Ralph Waldo Emerson, American poet, essayist, and transcendentalist

Gnosticism *(NAH-stih-sih-zim), noun*
The religious belief that salvation is attained through secret knowledge rather than through prayer, ritual, faith, divine grace, or good works.
Many of the key principles of Christianity were formed as a direct response to GNOSTICISM.

gorgonize *(GORE-guh-nize), verb*
To paralyze or mesmerize with one's looks or personality.
Even without her family's wealth and connections, Marla would likely GORGONIZE all the men who enter her orbit.

gormandize *(GORE-mun-dize), verb*
To eat like a glutton, as if one was starving.

We find GORMANDIZING on even the finest French cuisine to be quite tasteless and, therefore, to be avoided.

gossamer *(GAHSS-uh-muhr), adjective*
Something delicate, light, and flimsy that will flutter in the slightest breeze.

Fairies flitted among the flowers on GOSSAMER wings.

grandiloquent *(grand-EL-oh-kwent), adjective*
Having a pompous, overly inflated, hyperbolic, or pretentious way of presenting oneself in speech and mannerism.

The architect waxed GRANDILOQUENT about the visionary design of his new skyscraper.

granular *(GRAN-you-ler), adjective*
The ability to divide, organize, and search through something at a fine level of detail.

Julian's GRANULAR abilities allow him to extract the absolute best from among even the largest pile of uncut diamonds.

gratuitous *(grah-TOO-ih-tuss), adjective*
Unnecessary; inappropriately excessive; uncalled for.

"Being accused of making money by selling sex in Hollywood, home of the casting couch and the GRATUITOUS nude scene, is so rich with irony that it's a better subject for a comic novel than a column." – Anna Quindlen, American author and opinion columnist

gravitas *(gra-vih-TAS), adjective*
Behavior or manner that is dignified and serious, perhaps even a bit stiff, formal, and pompous.

The GRAVITAS with which Lionel viewed the Harvard-Yale football game was quite amusing to many of us.

gregarious *(greh-GARE-ee-us), adjective*
An extrovert; an outgoing person; one who is friendly and cheerful in nature.

"We are easy to manage, a **GREGARIOUS** people, / Full of sentiment, clever at mechanics, and we love our luxuries." – *Robinson Jeffers, American poet*

grievous *(GREE-vuhss), adjective*
Flagrant and outrageous; or, causing grief and great sorrow.
> *"Jealousy is a GRIEVOUS passion that jealously seeks what causes grief."*
> *– Franz Grillparzer, Austrian poet*

grouse *(GRAUSS), verb*
To complain or grumble about one's situation.
> *We decided not to return to the restaurant after the maître d' continuously GROUSED about the slovenliness of his wait staff.*

guaranty *(gar-an-TEE), noun*
The taking of responsibility by one person for another person's debts or other financial obligations. Also, the act of giving security.
> *"The Constitution is the sole source and GUARANTY of national freedom." – Calvin Coolidge*

guerrilla *(guh-RILL-uh), noun*
One who engages in warfare through small acts of harassment and sabotage.
> *With her keen eye for detail and authenticity, Lorissa has begun to wage a GUERRILLA war against stores that proffer knockoffs as legitimate couture.*

guile *(GILE), noun*
Deceitful cunning; trickery.

"Gaze no more in the bitter glass / The demons, with their subtle **GUILE**, / Lift up before us when they pass, / Or only gaze a little while." – *William Butler Yeats, Irish poet and dramatist*

gustatory *(GUSS-tuh-tore-ee), adjective*
Of the sense of taste.
> *"Food has it over sex for variety. Hedonistically, GUSTATORY possibilities are much broader than copulatory ones." – Joseph Epstein, American author and critic*

gryphon *(GRIFF-uhn), noun*
A mythical beast with the legs and body of a lion and the claws, head, and wings of an eagle.

"The GRYPHON'S claws were greatly prized, as they were reputed to change color in the presence of poison." – Richard Barber, British historian

guile *(GUY-ul), noun*
The act of being deliberately deceitful and treacherous, so as to gain advantage at someone else's expense.

I was amazed at the GUILE Richard displayed in going after my biggest account.

gyrating *(jye-RAY-ting), adjective*
Of a circular or spiral pattern.

When he first appeared on the Ed Sullivan *show, Elvis Presley's GYRATING hips during his act caused quite a stir.*

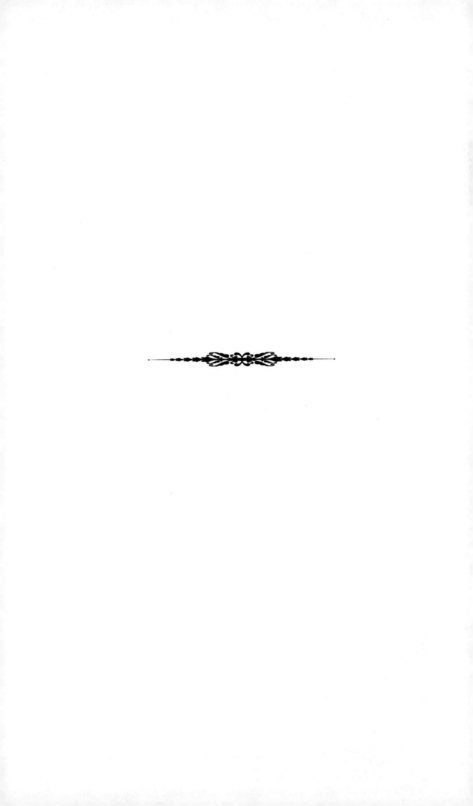

"The HAUGHTY sommelier, with his talismanic tasting cup and sometimes irritating self-assurance, is perceived more as the high priest of some arcane rite than as a dining room functionary paid to help you enjoy the evening."

———

Frank J. Prial, former *New York Times* wine columnist

H

habeas corpus *(HAY-bee-us-CORE-puss), noun*
A written order requiring a prisoner or person under arrest or confinement to be brought before a judge to assess whether the restraint of said person is lawful and proper.

> *Following the nightclub brawl, Chad and Wendell managed to receive a writ of HABEAS CORPUS only after their father called the authorities and reminded them of his social contacts.*

H

habile *(HAB-ill), adjective*
Skillful and able; handy.

> *Our HABILE gardener has helped render our topiary into the shapes of dollar and pound signs.*

habitude *(HAB-uh-tyood), noun*
Customary behavior or customary procedure.

> *Alistair's HABITUDE is for the servants to awake him just prior to noon.*

hagiography *(hag-ee-OG-ruh-fee), noun*
A biography that idealizes its subject.

> *The Van Gelders were disappointed with the volume written about their illustrious descendants because the book fell far short of being a HAGIOGRAPHY.*

halation *(hal-AYE-shun), noun*
A blurred image or ring of light caused by the reflection or dispersal of light.

> *The mysterious white ring he claims is a ghost is merely HALATION caused by the photographer's lighting.*

halcyon *(HAL-see-on), adjective*
Calm, peaceful, carefree, prosperous.

> *"It was the most HALCYON summer I ever spent." – Rick Bass, American author and environmental activist*

hapless *(HAP-liss), adjective*
Unlucky and unfortunate.

> *"Exile is the noble and dignified term, while a refugee is more HAPLESS." – Mary McCarthy, American author*

harangue *(ha-RANG), verb, noun*
Verbally accost; yell at; berate.

> *"But on that hot July day she breaks—HARANGUING strangers in the street." – Oliver Sacks, British neurologist*

harbinger *(HAR-bin-jer)*, *noun*
A forerunner or warning sign of a future event or trend.
> *The asteroid's shadow blotted out the sun as it speeded on a collision course with Earth, a HARBINGER of impending doom.*

harpy *(HAR-pee)*, *noun*
A greedy and predatory person; or, a scolding and shrewish woman.
> *"That HARPY Charlotte can't wait to get her claws into Bruce," Nancy observed.*

harry *(HAR-ee)*, *verb*
To torment with constant attacks.

> "At middle night great cats with silver claws, / Bodies of shadow and blind eyes like pearls, / Came up out of the hole, and red-eared hounds / With long white bodies came out of the air / Suddenly, and ran at them and **HARRIED** them." – *William Butler Yeats, Irish poet and dramatist*

haughty *(HAW-tee)*, *adjective*
Snobbish and arrogant.
> *"The HAUGHTY sommelier, with his talismanic tasting cup and sometimes irritating self-assurance, is perceived more as the high priest of some arcane rite than as a dining room functionary paid to help you enjoy the evening." – Frank J. Prial, former* New York Times *wine columnist*

haute couture *(OAT-koo-TOOR)*, *noun*
Highly fashionable clothing on the cutting edge of the latest design fads and trends.
> *"HAUTE COUTURE should be fun, foolish, and almost unwearable."*
> *– Christian Lacroix, French fashion designer*

haut monde *(oh-MAHND)*, *noun*
High society.

> "The literary wiseacres prognosticate in many languages, as they have throughout so many centuries, setting the stage for new **HAUT MONDE** in letters and making up the public's mind." – *Fannie Hurst, American novelist*

hearsay *(HEER-say), noun*
Information gathered from another that is not part of one's direct knowledge.

> *"My talk to thee must be how Benedick / Is sick in love with Beatrice. Of this matter / Is little Cupid's crafty arrow made, / That only wounds by HEARSAY." – William Shakespeare*

hedonism *(HEE-duh-niz-im), noun*
The nonstop pursuit of personal pleasure as one's primary goal.

> *"[Bad] taste supervenes upon good taste as a daring and witty HEDO-NISM. It makes the man of good taste cheerful, where before he ran the risk of being chronically frustrated." – Susan Sontag, American literary theorist, philosopher, and political activist*

hegemony *(hih-JEH-muhn-ee), noun*
Domination of a region or the entire world by a single nation, or the authority of one individual over an entire group.

> *Alison should not achieve HEGEMONY over the rest of us merely because her list of social contacts is slightly longer than ours.*

hellacious *(hel-AYE-shus), adjective*
Extremely brutal, violent, and severe.

> *Madison's foray into the corporate world was so HELLACIOUS that she quickly went back to being supported solely by her trust fund.*

herculean *(her-kyuh-LEE-uhn), adjective*
Of extraordinary power or difficulty. Often capitalized because the word alludes to Hercules.

> *"We found it a HERCULEAN effort not to chortle at the outlandish clothing of the nouveau riche attendees of our party," said Lillian. "How inappropriate to wear evening attire to an afternoon garden party!"*

heretic *(HER-eh-tik), noun*
A person who boldly, loudly, and publicly defies the conventions of a religion, society, culture, or set of beliefs.

> "The HERETIC is always better dead. And mortal eyes cannot distinguish the saint from the **HERETIC**." – *George Bernard Shaw, Irish playwright*

hermetic *(her-MET-ick), adjective*
Isolated, or unaffected by outside influences.
> *"Reality, whether approached imaginatively or empirically, remains a surface, HERMETIC."* – Samuel Beckett, Irish writer, dramatist, and poet

hiatus *(high-AY-tuss), noun*
An interruption or break.
> *Lorelei's coming-out party was a welcome HIATUS in our otherwise uneventful social calendar.*

hidebound *(HIDE-bound), adjective*
Inflexible and holding narrow opinions.
> *Wallace can be rather HIDEBOUND when pontificating on the virtues of classic Mercedes-Benz models versus the condition of the automobile company at present.*

hierarchy *(HIGH-uhr-ahr-key), noun*
A pecking order or ranking according to status or level of authority.
> *In the HIERARCHY of the military, a medical doctor, who is assigned the rank of captain but is not a military man, automatically outranks a lieutenant who may have years of battle experience.*

histrionics *(hiss-tree-AHN-iks), noun*
Over-the-top, unnecessarily dramatic behavior.
> *"Enough with the HISTRIONICS!" his mother scolded, immediately shutting off the flow of tears and silencing his bawling.*

hoary *(HOAR-ee), adjective*
Impressively old; ancient.
> *"Feminism has tried to dismiss the femme fatale as a misogynist libel, a HOARY cliché. But the femme fatale expresses women's ancient and eternal control of the sexual realm."* – Camille Paglia, American author, feminist, and social critic

hoi polloi *(HOY-puh-LOY), noun*
A pejorative term used to describe the masses or the common people.
> *"My practice is to ignore the pathetic wishes and desires of the HOI POLLOI,"* the governor said haughtily.

holarctic *(hole-ARK-tik), adjective*
Anything relating to the geographical distribution of animals in the Arctic region.

> *Our so-called Arctic safari was a bust. No one told us that, due to HOLARCTIC conditions, we would find no polar bears near our encampment.*

holistic *(ho-LISS-tik), adjective*
Refers to medical practices that treat the whole person and not just a specific organ, condition, or disease.

> *Marsha's HOLISTIC approach to healing involves channeling energy through crystals.*

homage *(HOM-ij), noun*
Respect paid and deference shown to a superior or other person one admires, fears, or wishes to emulate or praise.

> *Gary took black and white photos with a non-digital camera in HOMAGE to Ansel Adams, whose works he greatly admired.*

homeopathy *(HOME-ee-oh-path-ee), noun*
The medical practice of giving patients minerals, metals, herbs, and other bioactive compounds in extremely diluted form.

> *Most modern scientists believe the effectiveness of HOMEOPATHY in some cases is due mainly to the placebo effect.*

homeostatis *(ho-me-oh-STAY-sis), noun*
A dynamic system in which balance between input and output has been achieved, so no net changes take place.

> *When HOMEOSTATIS is achieved in a sealed biosphere, the animals and plants can live without outside air, food, or water.*

homogenous *(ho-mo-JEAN-yus), adjective*
Consistent in composition or uniform in structure.

> *"By the mere act of watching television, a heterogeneous society could engage in a purely HOMOGENEOUS activity." – William J. Donnelly, American media critic*

honorific *(on-err-IF-ik), adjective*
A tribute or reward given in an effort to honor someone as a sign of deep respect.

> *Lifetime achievement awards aren't for any single work, but an HONORIFIC for long service and a track record of excellence.*

hubris *(HYOO-briss), noun*
To possess pride, arrogance, or conceit not justified by reality.
> *Those who accuse us of HUBRIS are simply unaware of the efforts our families have made to perfect our bloodlines.*

humanism *(HEW-man-iz-um), noun*
The philosophy or belief that the highest ideals of human existence can be fulfilled without regard to religion or supernatural intervention.
> *"The four characteristics of HUMANISM are curiosity, a free mind, belief in good taste, and belief in the human race." – E. M. Forster, English novelist*

humectant *(hue-MEK-tant), noun*
A substance that absorbs moisture or retains water.
> *Sorbitol, a HUMECTANT, is used in the processing of dried fruit.*

hygroscopic *(high-grow-SKOP-ick), adjective*
Capable of absorbing moisture from the air.
> *Prescription pills are often packed with a container of HYGROSCOPIC material to keep the drugs dry.*

hyperbaric *(hi-per-BARE-ik), adjective*
Related to artificially high atmospheric pressure, used to treat certain diseases.
> *Divers who ascend to the surface too rapidly may be placed in a HYPERBARIC chamber to prevent the bends.*

hyperbole *(high-PERR-buh-lee), noun*
An over-exaggeration made for effect.

> "The final key to the way I promote is bravado. I play to people's fantasies. People may not always think big themselves, but they can still get very excited by those who do. That's why a little **HYPERBOLE** never hurts." – *Donald Trump, American entrepreneur*

Hyperborean *(high-per-BORE-ee-an), noun*
A person or animal who lives at or near the North Pole.
> *The polar bear, one of the great HYPERBOREANS, is in danger of extinction as the melting of the polar cap makes the ice floes on which they live disappear.*

hypercritical *(high-purr-KRIT-ih-kuhl), adjective*
Excessively or meticulously critical.

> *"Good writers have two things in common: they would rather be understood than admired, and they do not write for hairsplitting and HYPERCRITICAL readers." – Friedrich Nietzche, German philosopher*

hypnopompic *(hip-nuh-PAHM-pick), adjective*
Having to do with the semiconscious state that precedes wakefulness.

> *With all of her partying at exclusive clubs, Madison spends most of her life in a HYPNOPOMPIC state.*

hypothecation *(hi-POTH-ih-KAY-shun), noun*
The practice of using property or other assets as the collateral for a loan.

> *Buying stock on margin is a useful form of HYPOTHECATION that encourages unsophisticated individual investors to buy more stock than they can afford.*

hypothesis *(high-POTH-uh-sis), noun*
A principle derived from limited evidence, seen as sensible based on an analysis of available data, but not proven to the point where it is an accepted theory, rule, or law.

> *"In order to shake a HYPOTHESIS, it is sometimes not necessary to do anything more than push it as far as it will go." – Denis Diderot, French philosopher*

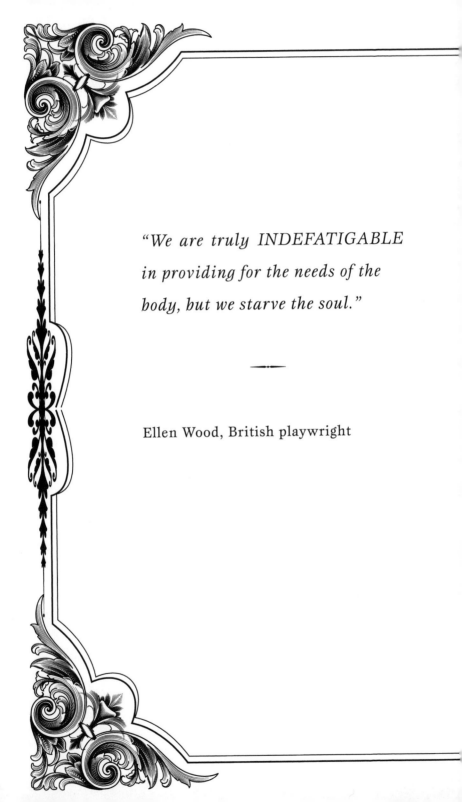

"*We are truly* INDEFATIGABLE *in providing for the needs of the body, but we starve the soul.*"

Ellen Wood, British playwright

I

iconoclast *(eye-KAHN-uh-clast)*, *noun*

An individual who is contrarian in thought, rebellious in spirit, oppositional, and who applies himself to battling established institutions, existing governments, religious doctrine, and popular notions and beliefs.

> *The late George Carlin saw the role of the comic in society as one of ICONOCLAST.*

ideologue *(EYE-dee-oh-log)*, *noun*

A person who rigidly adheres to an ideology with a closed mind regarding other points of view.

> *"An IDEOLOGUE may be defined as a mad intellectual." – Clifton Fadiman, American critic*

ignominious *(ig-no-MIN-ee-us)*, *adjective*

Marked by failure or humiliation in public.

> *After his IGNOMINIOUS defeat in the election, Frank never ran for Congress again.*

imbroglio *(im-BRO-lee-oh)*, *noun*

Colloquially referred to as a "sticky situation"—a predicament that is difficult to get out of.

> *Our inability to decide which New Year's Eve party to attend created an IMBROGLIO that disrupted our social calendar for months.*

immure *(ih-MYOOR)*, *verb*

To confine, imprison, or enclose behind walls.

> *Whitney remained IMMURED in her room as she pondered the itinerary for her luxury vacation to Italy.*

immutable *(im-MYOO-tuh-bull)*, *adjective*

Unable, or unwilling, to change.

> *"I don't know what IMMUTABLE differences exist between men and women apart from differences in their genitals." – Naomi Weisstein, American feminist*

impalpable *(im-PAL-puh-bull)*, *adjective*

Difficult to understand easily; or, intangible.

> "The soul is so **IMPALPABLE**, so often useless, and sometimes such a nuisance, that I felt no more emotion on losing it than if, on a stroll, I had mislaid my visiting card." – *Charles Baudelaire, French poet, critic, and translator*

imparity *(ihm-PAR-ih-tee), noun*
Inequality or disparity.
> *There is little, if any, IMPARITY between the chateaubriand offered at the two bistros.*

impecunious *(im-puh-KYOON-ee-us), adjective*
To be poor or broke; to have little or no money.
> *Alex has been raving about his IMPECUNIOUS state ever since his trust fund was cut from $25,000 to $20,000 per month.*

implausible *(im-PLAWZ-ih-bull), adjective*
Difficult to believe; highly unlikely to be true.
> *"At first glance, most famous fairy tales seem so IMPLAUSIBLE and irrelevant to contemporary life that their survival is hard to understand."*
> *– Alison Lurie, American novelist and academic*

implicit *(im-PLIH-set), adjective*
Something that is understood or implied but not stated directly.
> *"The vanity of men, a constant insult to women, is also the ground for the IMPLICIT feminine claim of superior sensitivity and morality." – Patricia Meyer Spacks, American literary critic*

importunate *(ihm-PORE-chuh-nitt), adjective*
Urgent and persistent in solicitation, to the point of annoyance.
> *"Sisters are always drying their hair. / Locked into rooms, alone, / They pose at the mirror, shoulders bare, / Trying this way and that their hair, / Or fly IMPORTUNATE down the stair / To answer the telephone."*
> *– Phyllis McGinley, American poet*

imprecation *(IM-pre-kay-shun), noun*
A curse spoken aloud.
> *Thomas muttered IMPRECATIONS as he circled the airfield, waiting for clearance to land his Airbus 380.*

improvidence *(im-PRAH-vih-dense), noun*
A rash action performed without careful consideration or deliberation.
> *"This made him think of all the nights . . . spending his youth with the casual IMPROVIDENCE of a millionaire." – Richard Matheson, American science fiction writer*

impugn *(ihm-PYOON), verb*
To attack as false or wrong.

"I do not IMPUGN the motives of any one opposed to me. It is no pleasure to me to triumph over any one." –Abraham Lincoln

impute *(im-PYOOT), verb*
To attribute something, to assign responsibility or blame.

> "The sin I **IMPUTE** to each frustrute ghost / Is—the unlit lamp and the ungirt loin, / Though the end in sight was a vice, I say." – *Robert Browning, British poet and playwright*

incipient *(in-SIH-pee-ent), adjective*
In the early stages of development; developing but not fully formed.
The chef's INCIPIENT cuisine already surpasses the fare of other, more established, culinary artists.

incommensurable *(in-co-MEN-ser-uh-bull), adjective*
Two things that cannot be measured or judged by the same standards.
"Two men who perceive the same situation differently but employ the same vocabulary in its discussion speak from INCOMMENSURABLE viewpoints." – Thomas Kuhn, American philosopher

incongruous *(in-KAHNG-grew-us), adjective*
Describes something that does not belong in its current place, setting, or role; out of place; not fitting in.
"The taste for quotations (and for the juxtaposition of INCONGRUOUS quotations) is a Surrealist taste." – Susan Sontag, American literary theorist, philosopher, and political activist

incontrovertible *(in-kahn-trah-VER-tih-bull), adjective*
Beyond question or dispute.
"Some minds are as little logical or argumentative as nature; they can offer no reason or "guess," but they exhibit the solemn and INCONTROVERTIBLE fact." – Henry David Thoreau, American author and transcendentalist

inculcate *(IN-kul-kate), transitive verb*
To impress an idea or belief upon someone by repeating it to that person over and over until the idea is firmly lodged in his brain.
New cult members are quickly INCULCATED with the cult leader's beliefs and world view.

inculpate *(in-KOOL-pate), verb*
To incriminate, blame, or charge with a crime.

Thanks to our connections, none of us were INCULPATED in the night-club melee.

indefatigable *(in-deh-fah-TEE-gah-bull), adjective*
Capable of continuing along one's current course of action without wavering, tiring, or faltering.

"We are truly INDEFATIGABLE in providing for the needs of the body, but we starve the soul." – Ellen Wood, British playwright

indite *(in-DITE), verb*
To write or compose a literary work.

"But if, both for your love and skill, your name / You seek to nurse at fullest breasts of Fame, / Stella behold, and then begin to INDITE." – Sir Philip Sidney, English courtier, soldier, and poet

ineffable *(in-EF-uh-bull), adjective*
Something so fantastic, incredible, or difficult-to-grasp it cannot be described in words.

Poet Ezra Pound wrote of "the infinite and INEFFABLE quality of the British empire."

ineluctable *(In-el-LUCK-tah-bull), adjective*
Unavoidable, inevitable, with a sense of being unfortunate, sad, or even tragic.

Our inability to procure Pratesi linens for our Colorado ski lodge created an INELUCTABLE sadness among the members of our family.

inexorable *(in-eks-ZOR-ah-bull), adjective*
Inevitable; unavoidable; relentless; persistent; unstoppable.

"I know enough to know that most of the visible signs of aging are the result of the INEXORABLE victory of gravity over tissue." – Isaac Asimov, Russian-born American author and biochemist

inextricably *(in-eks-TRIK-uh-blee), adverb*
Something that is strongly linked to something else, with the bond between quite difficult to break.

"At its best, [Japanese cooking] is INEXTRICABLY meshed with aesthetics, with religion, with tradition and history." – M. F. K. Fisher, American author

inference *(IN-fer-ence), noun*
The process of reaching a logical conclusion by examining and analyzing the evidence.

> *Watson solved cases through INFERENCE, while Sherlock Holmes was seemingly gifted with flashes of brilliant insight.*

inimical *(ih-NIM-ih-kull), adjective*
Something working in opposition to your goal; having a harmful effect, particularly on an enterprise or endeavor.

Clarissa's decorating sense is INIMICAL to producing a successful soiree.

innocuous *(ih-NAHK-yew-us), adjective*
Not harmful or offensive; innocent, incidental, and hardly noticeable.

> *"I know those little phrases that seem so INNOCUOUS and, once you let them in, pollute the whole of speech." – Samuel Beckett, Irish writer, dramatist, and poet*

inscrutable *(in-SKROO-tuh-bull), adjective*
Mysterious and not easy to understand.

> *"I suppose I now have the reputation of being an INSCRUTABLE dipsomaniac. One woman here originated the rumour that I am extremely lazy and will never do or finish anything." – James Joyce, Irish author and playwright*

insouciant *(in-SOO-see-unt), adjective*
Acting as if one has not a care in the world; free of worry and angst.

> *We are never INSOUCIANT about our wealth because we must work at all times to ensure its protection.*

insular *(INN-suh-ler), adjective*
Self-contained and therefore isolated from the world and unaffected by outside influences, usually to one's detriment.

> *The Pricewaters moved from the family's tradition enclave to a more INSULAR compound further up the coast.*

insuperable *(in-SOO-per-uh-bull), adjective*
Not possible to overcome or surmount.

> *"Conceit is an INSUPERABLE obstacle to all progress." Ellen Terry, British actress*

intelligentsia *(in-tell-ih-GENT-see-uh), noun*
The class of people who are cultured, educated, intellectual, and interested in art and literature.

"You see these gray hairs? Well, making whoopee with the INTELLI-GENTSIA was the way I earned them." – Dorothy Parker, American author and poet

intemperate *(in-TEM-prit), adjective*
Refers to a person who indulges his own whims and fancies without regard to other people's feelings or inconvenience.
"Certainly it was ordained as a scourge upon the pride of human wisdom, that the wisest of us all, should thus outwit ourselves, and eternally forego our purposes in the INTEMPERATE act of pursuing them." – Laurence Sterne, Irish-born English novelist and Anglican clergyman

interminably *(in-TUR-min-uh-blee), adverb*
Seemingly without end or going on for an indeterminate period of time.

"The body dies; the body's beauty lives. / So evenings die, in their green going, / A wave, **INTERMINABLY** flowing." – *Wallace Stevens, American Modernist poet*

interpolate *(in-TER-poh-late), verb*
To introduce something—often something unnecessary—between other things or parts.
Dexter could not help but continuously INTERPOLATE unnecessary criticism into the discussion of the latest Parisian designs.

interpose *(in-ter-POZ), verb*
To aggressively insert your unsolicited opinion, assistance, or presence into a situation where it is not particularly wanted.
"I hope I am not INTERPOSING," Eileen said as she walked in on our meeting—which of course, she was.

intractable *(in-TRACK-tuh-bull), adjective*
Difficult to control or manage.
"It is precisely here, where the writer fights with the raw, the INTRAC-TABLE, that poetry is born." – Doris Lessing, British author

intransigent *(in-TRANZ-ih-gent), adjective*
Stubborn; refusing to consider opinions other than one's own.
"Lamont stared for a moment in frustration but Burt's expression was a clearly INTRANSIGENT one now." – Isaac Asimov, Russian-born American author and biochemist

intrinsic *(in-TRIN-zick), adjective*
Of, or related to, something's essential nature.

> *"We are the men of INTRINSIC value, who can strike our fortunes out of ourselves, whose worth is independent of accidents in life, or revolutions in government: we have heads to get money, and hearts to spend it." – George Farquhar, Irish dramatist*

inurement *(inn-UR-meant), noun*
Acceptance without resistance or fighting back of punishment, poor treatment, or unpleasant circumstances or conditions.

> *"Perhaps others might respond to this treatment with INUREMENT,"*
> *Eloise hissed, "but I will buy my diamonds at another boutique from this point forward."*

invective *(inn-VEK-tiv), noun*
Criticism or negative observations expressed in the strongest, harshest possible terms.

> "The art of **INVECTIVE** resembles the art of boxing. Very few fights are won with the straight left. It is too obvious, and it can be too easily countered." – *Gilbert Highet, Scottish-born American biographer and essayist*

inveigle *(in-VAY-gull), verb*
To convince or persuade someone through trickery, dishonesty, or flattery.

> *Craig INVEIGLED the dean to allow him to graduate even though he failed to meet the foreign language requirement of the university.*

inveterate *(in-VET-uh-rett), adjective*
A pattern of behavior or habit that never changes.

> *"Take all the garden spills, / INVETERATE, / prodigal spender / just as summer goes." – Hilda Doolittle, American poet and memoirist*

invidious *(in-VID-ee-us), adjective*
Designed to give offense or to create ill will.

> *"In the name of all lechers and boozers I most solemnly protest against the INVIDIOUS distinction made to our prejudice." – Aldous Huxley, British author and humanist*

inviolate *(inn-VY-oh-late), adjective*
Without restriction, violation, supervision, or fear of punishment.
"INVIOLATE, he could rupture wires, mangle flaps, destroy the balance of the ship." – Richard Matheson, American science fiction writer

invious *(IN-vee-uhs), adjective*
Unwalked, and thus, pristine.
The Wallenstones' new compound contains many INVIOUS tracts perfect for hiking or fox hunting.

irascible *(ih-RASS-uh-bull), adjective*
Easily irritated or annoyed; prone to losing one's temper; quick to anger.
"I have never known anyone worth a damn who wasn't IRASCIBLE." – Ezra Pound, American expatriate poet

iridescent *(ear-ih-DES-uhnt), adjective*
Showing luminous colors that seem to change depending upon the angle from which they are viewed.
"We passed . . . broken shells and the IRIDESCENT film of egg splatter reflected under streetlights where a battle had taken place." – Jeffrey Ford, American fantasy author

irremediable *(ihr-ree-MEE-dee-uh-bull), adjective*
Impossible to cure or remedy.
Sylvia's outdated concept of couture is completely IRREMEDIABLE.

isochronous *(EYE-so-krone-us), adjective*
Occurring consistently at regular intervals.
The ticking of a clock is ISOCHRONOUS, but the arrival of the elevator at different floors is not.

isolationism *(eye-so-LAY-shin-iz-um), noun*
A foreign policy in which a country deliberately keeps its relationships and interactions with other nations to a bare minimum, effectively isolating itself from world affairs.
In the early twentieth century, American ISOLATIONISM stopped the U.S. from joining the League of Nations.

iteration *(ih-ter-AYE-shun), noun*
The process of performing a series of instructions or steps repeatedly; also refers to one repetition of those repeated steps.
"Thou hast damnable ITERATION, and art indeed able to corrupt a saint." – William Shakespeare

"The tradition I cherish is the ideal this country was built upon, the concept of religious pluralism, of a plethora of opinions, of tolerance and not the JIHAD. Religious war, pooh. The war is between those who trust us to think and those who believe we must merely be led."

———

Anna Quindlen, American author and opinion columnist

jactitation *(jak-ti-TAY-shun), noun*
A false boast, especially one that is harmful to others.
> *Beatrice tried to impress her classmates by telling them her last name was Kennedy. However, her JACTITATION was discovered and her peers returned to ignoring her.*

jaundiced *(JAWN-dist), adjective*
Demonstrating prejudice, due to envy or resentment.
> *The Blythingtons' view of our dinner parties is JAUNDICED by the fact that our personal chef is superior to theirs.*

jaunt *(JAWNT), noun*
A short journey taken for pleasure.
> *Nicole plans to take a JAUNT across the southern tip of Africa next year.*

jawbone *(JAW-bon), verb*
To attempt to get someone to do something through persuasion rather than by force.
> *No matter how much he JAWBONED, Karl could not get Alison to sell her stock prior to the unveiling of the company's disastrous new line of parvenu fashion.*

jejune *(jih-JUNE), adjective*
Thoughts and actions that are not well thought out or fully formed; a poor performance or inferior work.
> *Samantha snidely informed Blake that her JEJUNE entertaining efforts might someday grow to maturity.*

jeremiad *(jer-uh-MY-uhd), noun*
A document or speech in which the author bitterly rails against the injustices of society or warns of impending death, destruction, or doom.
> *The Unabomber's Manifesto was an intelligently written JEREMIAD.*

jihad *(gee-HOD), noun*
Striving toward an important goal; in modern usage, a holy war conducted in the name of Islam.
> *"The tradition I cherish is the ideal this country was built upon, the concept of religious pluralism, of a plethora of opinions, of tolerance and not the JIHAD. Religious war, pooh. The war is between those who trust us to think and those who believe we must merely be led." – Anna Quindlen, American author and opinion columnist*

jingoism *(GIN-go-iz-um)*, *noun*
Extreme nationalism, backed up by the explicit or implied threat of military force; more broadly, extreme enthusiasm and support for an idea or position without being open to contrary arguments or notions.

We cannot countenance JINGOISM, especially since it has such a negative impact on overseas markets.

J

jinn *(JIN)*, *noun*
A mythical creature created from fire long before man inhabited the Earth.

Failing in their rebellion against God, the JINN were banished to the deserts.

jocose *(joe-KOSS)*, *adjective*
Humorous, playful, and characterized by good humor.

The pony's JOCOSE antics marked it for a career in polo, rather than on the racetrack.

jocund *(JOE-kund)*, *adjective*
Having a lust for life; possessing a positive attitude and desire to enjoy life to the fullest.

Ron's JOCUND façade shattered when he found himself the victim of identity theft.

journeyman *(JUR-nee-man)*, *noun*
A person who, although not a top master of his profession, has become extremely competent, through long years of practice, at a particular craft or skill.

"So this is happiness, / that **JOURNEYMAN**." – *Anne Sexton, American poet and author*

juggernaut *(JUG-er-nawt)*, *noun*
A large, overpowering, destructive force.

Once he begins arguing about the superiority of Maseratis, Jefferson becomes a JUGGERNAUT, capable of deflating anyone else's arguments.

jurisprudence *(joor-iss-PROO-dense), noun*
The philosophy and methodology behind the practice of law.
> *The study of JURISPRUDENCE was interminably dull to John; he longed to work with real clients and real court cases.*

juvenilia *(joo-vuh-NILL-yuh), noun*
Early work by a creative artist, typically produced when the artist or writer was young.
> *Lorna turned toward the stock market and away from poetry after we read her JUVENILIA and laughed uproariously.*

juxtaposition *(juhk-stuh-puh-ZISH-uhn), noun*
The observation of the differences between two items being compared side by side.

> "A manic **JUXTAPOSITION** turned Hill House into a place of despair."
> – *Shirley Jackson, American author*

kabbalism *(KAH-bah-liz-um), noun*
A Jewish mystical tradition, based on revelation instead of reason, in which mystical feats can be performed by manipulating the letters of the Hebrew alphabet.
> *Through meditation, KABBALISM enables practitioners to become one with God.*

kaffeeklatsch *(CAW-fee-klatch), noun*
An informal social gathering, typically including coffee and gossip.
> *Jeanette is not welcome at our KAFFEEKLATSCH because she refuses to gossip about her social contacts.*

kapellmeister *(kuh-PELL-my-ster), noun*
The director of a choir or orchestra.
> *Ever since the Prithingtons hired a personal KAPELLMEISTER for their Christmas parties, everyone else has had to follow suit.*

kelvin *(KEL-vin), noun*
A temperature scale in which absolute zero is zero degrees, and there are no negative values.
> *When we questioned Rachel about her purse, suggesting that it is a knock-off, she gave us a stare cold enough to measure on the KELVIN scale.*

kenning *(KEN-ing), noun*
A metaphorical compound word or phrase, used often in epic poetry.
Cliff's letter to Natasha included such KENNINGS as "pearl-eyed dove" and "crinkly gowned angel." It's no wonder she broke up with him soon after.

kerning *(KER-ning), noun*
In typography, the amount of spacing between letters in a word or line of type.
If the KERNING is too large or too small, words are difficult to read.

K

kibosh *(kih-BOSH), noun*
Something that serves to stop something else.
Father put the KIBOSH on my plans to extend my summer trip to Europe by another three months.

kinesiology *(kih-nee-see-OL-uh-jee), noun*
The science of muscles and their function, physical movement, and muscular development.
As a body builder, he studied both nutrition and KINESIOLOGY.

kismet *(KIHZ-met), noun*
Fate or destiny.
Elaine's parvenu background hardly seemed destined to make her part of our group, but KISMET has made her an important social contact.

kitsch *(KIHCH), noun*
Art, artifacts, or other objects of a cheap or junky nature produced by the popular culture.
His room was filled with KITSCH: lava lamps, Farrah Fawcett and Cheryl Tiegs posters, and plastic models of Frankenstein and Dracula.

knavish *(NAY-vish), adjective*
Untrustworthy, dishonest, and mischievous.
Despite, or perhaps because of, his KNAVISH behavior, Jonathan is always a success at our society balls.

knell *(NELL), noun*
The sound of a bell, especially when rung solemnly at a funeral.

"They are of sick and diseased imaginations who would toll the world's **KNELL** so soon." – *Henry David Thoreau, American author and transcendentalist*

kowtow *(KOW-tow), verb*
To give in to someone's every wish; to grovel and behave in a subservient manner.

Amy told Andrew that she was sick and tired of KOWTOWING to his every need.

kraken *(KRAH-ken), noun*
A gigantic creature, somewhat like the Loch Ness Monster, reputedly sighted off the coast of Norway.

Most of the KRAKEN reported as washed up on beaches were probably giant squid.

Kwanzaa *(KWAN-zah), noun*
An African holiday observed by many African Americans from December 26 to January 1.

We feel we are doing our part to foster multiculturalism by allowing the stray KWANZAA decoration at our Christmas parties.

kyphosis *(ki-FOE-sis), noun*
Excessive curvature of the spine suffered by hunchbacks.

After William's father forced him to help out the family gardener, William complained for weeks afterward that the outdoor work gave him KYPHOSIS.

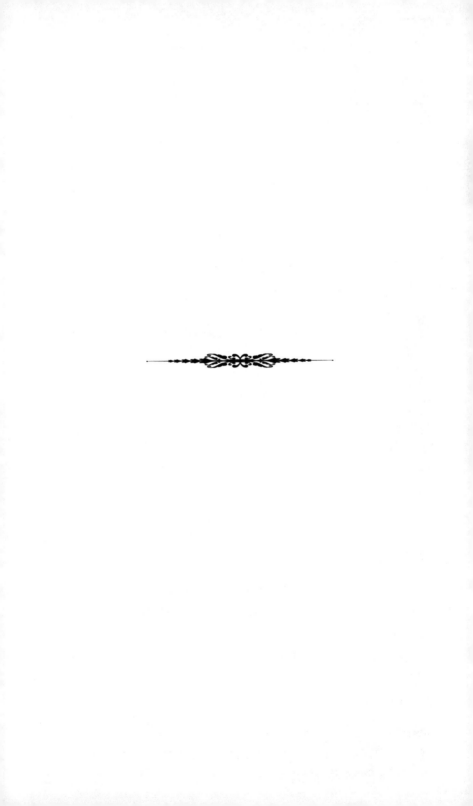

"*I fear the popular notion of success stands in direct opposition in all points to the real and wholesome success. One adores public opinion, the other, private opinion; one, fame, the other, desert; one, feats, the other, humility; one, LUCRE, the other, love.*"

———

Ralph Waldo Emerson, American poet, essayist, and transcendentalist

L

labanotation *(la-bah-no-TAY-shun), noun*
A nomenclature used to choreograph ballets, modern dance, and other performances so the dancers can follow the steps.

> *Even with the best-available LABANOTATION, Walker was unable to adequately perform a Viennese waltz at Natasha's coming-out party.*

L

labyrinth *(LAH-buh-rinth), noun*
A mazelike series of connected tunnels and passages through which it is difficult to find one's way.

> *He ran, terrified, as the enraged Minotaur chased him throughout the LABYRINTH.*

lachrymose *(LAH-krih-mose), adjective*
Describes someone who cries at the drop of a hat.

> *She was so LACHRYMOSE, she cried at commercials for long-distance phone companies.*

lackadaisical *(lack-uh-DAY-zih-kuhl), adjective*
Lazy and indolent; lacking determination.

> *No matter how many times a week her father allows her to go on a spending spree, Millicent is never LACKADAISACAL about her trips to Cartier.*

laconic *(luh-KON-ik), adjective*
Being a person of few words; expressing oneself with an economy of words.

> *Harold may be LACONIC, but when he does speak, he is certainly worth listening to.*

lactation *(lak-TAY-shun), noun*
The production of milk from the breasts of a mother mammal so her young can feed by sucking on the nipple.

> *When mother took us to visit the farm on one part of our property, she shielded our young eyes from the LACTATION of the various animals.*

laggard *(LAG-uhrd), noun or adjective*
A person who loiters; sluggish and reacting slowly.

> *"Reviewers . . . must normally function as huff-and-puff artists blowing LAGGARD theatergoers stageward." – Walter Kerr, American theater critic*

lagniappe *(lan-YAP)*, *noun*
An unexpected bonus gift or extra benefit; the icing on the cake.
Frederick would have bought the Porsche Panamera, even without the LAGNIAPPE of a free voice-activated navigation system.

laissez faire *(lah-zay-FAIR)*, *noun*
The belief that government should not interfere in economic affairs, but should instead let the economy take its natural course.
Our family began to place most of its money in hedge funds when we became convinced that the government intended to forego LAISSEZ FAIRE and take a more active part in the nation's financial system.

lambaste *(lam-BAST)*, *verb*
To berate or criticize harshly, especially in an unkind way.
We LAMBASTED Marla for not visiting Comme des Garçons during her recent weekender to Beijing.

lammergeyer *(LAM-er-GEE-er)*, *noun*
A large black bird of the vulture family.
"The world is just that LAMMERGEYER, or bearded vulture, in the sky." – *Pico Iyer, British-born essayist of Indian descent*

lampoon *(LAM-poon)*, *noun or verb*
A mean-spirited satire directed at a person or institution; or, the act of submitting someone to a mean-spirited satire.
We LAMPOONED the nouveau riche attendees of our April Fool's Day party simply by dressing in the same overwrought couture favored by parvenus.

languid *(LANG-gwid)*, *adjective*
Characterized by weakness and fatigue; or, lacking spirit and animation.

"In doing good, we are generally cold, and **LANGUID**, and sluggish; and of all things afraid of being too much in the right." – *Edmund Burke, Anglo-Irish statesman, orator, and author*

lapping *(LAH-ping), noun*
The practice of falsifying accounting records to conceal a shortage caused by theft or loss, usually by posting a financial transaction to an accounting period other than the one during which it actually took place.

Even after Skyler was indicted, he could not accept that LAPPING was an objectionable practice.

largesse *(lar-JESS), noun*
The generous bestowal of gifts; or, generosity in general.

"A LARGESS universal, like the sun, / His liberal eye doth give to everyone, / Thawing cold fear." – William Shakespeare

lascivious *(luh-SIV-ee-us), adjective*
Interested in and eager to engage in sexual activity; sexual in nature.

"An impersonal and scientific knowledge of the structure of our bodies is the surest safeguard against prurient curiosity and **LASCIVIOUS** gloating." – *Marie Carmichael Stopes, British scientist and birth-control pioneer*

lassitude *(LAS-ih-tood), noun*
Having little energy or motivation; weariness.

"We know what boredom is: it is a dull / Impatience or a fierce velleity, / A champing wish, stalled by our **LASSITUDE**, / To make or do." – *Richard Wilbur, American poet*

latency *(LAY-ten-see), noun*
A period of dormancy that precedes a period of great growth or action.

We knew that Abigail's focus on extremely liberal causes was merely a LATENCY that would end with her focus solely on charitable giving to the proper charities.

latifundia *(lah-ti-FUN-dee-uh), noun*
A large estate, plantation, or farm run by wealthy owners and staffed with underpaid or semi-servile workers.
Billings argued that his family's sugar cane plantation in the Caribbean is not a LATIFUNDIA because the factory pays its workers what is considered a living wage for the country.

laudable *(LAW-duh-bull), adjective*
Commendable; deserving of praise.
Rebecca's decision to tell her mother that she lost the emerald brooch she borrowed without permission was LAUDABLE.

legerdemain *(le-juhr-duh-MAYN), noun*
Magic tricks; or, generally speaking, trickery and deception.
The Wilkinsons are one of the few of our families whose initial wealth did not come as a result of financial LEGERDEMAIN.

lethargic *(luh-THAHR-jihk), adjective*
Drowsy and sluggish; lacking vigor.
"Great talents, by the rust of long disuse, / Grow LETHARGIC and shrink from what they were." – Ovid, Roman poet

levant *(leh-VANT), noun*
The countries on the eastern coast of the Mediterranean Sea.
Ties between Western Europe and the LEVANT were first established during the Crusades.

leverage *(LEH-veh-ridge), noun*
Possessing an advantage or extra degree of influence in a given situation.
With his family's connections, Eldridge required no LEVERAGE to obtain a sinecure in the financial industry.

leviathan *(le-VY-ah-thun), adjective*
A gigantic creature, structure, or thing, awe-inspiring in its sheer size.
"Wilson looked out through the window at the LEVIATHAN glitter of the terminal." – Richard Matheson, American science fiction writer

levity *(LEHV-ih-tee), noun*
Lack of appropriate seriousness; or, inconstant in nature.

> "Love, which is the essence of God, is not for **LEVITY**, but for the total worth of man." – *Ralph Waldo Emerson, American poet, essayist, and transcendentalist*

lexicon *(LEK-sih-kahn), noun*
The language or vocabulary of a specialized discipline or profession.
> *"In the LEXICON of lip-smacking, an epicure is fastidious in his choice and enjoyment of food, just a soupçon more expert than a gastronome."*
> *– William Safire, American journalist and presidential speechwriter*

liaison *(lee-ay-ZAWHN), noun*
An adulterous relationship; or, a kind of illicit sexual relationship.
> *LIAISONS are much more common within our group than are stable marriages.*

libation *(lye-BAY-shun), noun*
An alcoholic beverage consumed at social gatherings, parties, and celebrations.
> *With the LIBATIONS flowing freely, each member of the winning team felt compelled to make a drunken speech.*

libertine *(LIB-er-teen), noun, adjective*
Licentious and free of moral restraint; or, a person so characterized.
> *"It is easier to make a saint out of a LIBERTINE than out of a prig."*
> *– George Santayana, author and philosopher*

libration *(ly-BRAY-shun), noun*
The oscillation of Earth's moon around its axis.
> *LIBRATIONS are caused by changes in the intensity of Earth's gravitational pull on the moon.*

licentious *(ly-SEN-shus), adjective*
Promiscuous; slutty; someone who is sexually uninhibited and free.
> *Janine's LICENTIOUS behavior was really a cry for attention, the school psychologist was convinced.*

lien *(LEAN), noun*
A creditor's right to have debts paid out of the debtor's property, if necessary by selling it.

It's sad that we, at times, must place LIENS on our servants' automobiles, but that is why they are the servers and we the "servees."

Lilliputian *(lil-ee-PEW-shun), adjective*
Small in stature; tiny in comparison to one's peers.
Jules Vern's LILLIPUTIAN appearance made people treat him like a child.

limpid *(LIM-pid), adjective*
Clear and transparent; free from obscurity.
The Motsingers are fond of saying that they are capable of eschewing all of the most LIMPID tax dodges.

lineage *(LIN-ee-ij), noun*
Ancestry; your family tree.
We still consider Rachel nouveau riche because her family can only trace its American LINEAGE to the mid-ninteenth century.

liquidity *(lih-KWI-dih-tee), noun*
The relative ease with which a person can sell an asset.
Despite a firm belief in wealth LIQUIDITY, Dotson continues to buy such depreciable items as yachts and Porsches.

lissome *(LISS-um), adjective*
Lithe; supple; flexible.
Moira acquired her LISSOME frame from years of swimming in her family's Olympic-sized pool.

litany *(LIT-n-ee), noun*
A prolonged and boring account.

"With the supermarket as our temple and the singing commercial as our **LITANY**, are we likely to fire the world with an irresistible vision of America's exalted purpose and inspiring way of life?" – *Adlai Stevenson, American politician*

literati *(lih-ter-AH-tee), noun*
The segment of society comprised of learned or literary men and women.

We attract the LITERATI because of our constantly carefree and exciting exploits.

lithe *(LIthE), adjective*
Having a body and/or mind that is limber, flexible, and supple.
> *"The coconut trees, LITHE and graceful, crowd the beach . . . like a minuet of slender elderly virgins adopting flippant poses." – William Manchester, American historian*

litigious *(lih-TIJ-us), adjective*
Readily inclined to take someone to court; or, very argumentative.
> *"Our wrangling lawyers . . . are so LITIGIOUS and busy here on earth, that I think they will plead their clients' causes hereafter,—some of them in hell." – Robert Burton, English scholar and vicar at Oxford University*

liturgy *(LIH-tur-jee), noun*
The performance of a Christian religious service in a church.
> *During the LITURGY, the singing of the Christmas hymns filled the church with the sound of joy.*

livid *(LIHV-id), adjective*
Enraged or extremely angry.
> *Jennifer was LIVID when we suggested that her new outfit was three weeks out of date.*

locution *(low-KEW-shin), noun*
A person's manner and style of speaking.
> *Neil prides himself on his precise LOCUTION, but some of the guys think he sounds rather prissy.*

logy *(LOW-gee), adjective*
Characterized by lethargy and sluggishness.

> "To be scared is such a release from all the **LOGY** weight of procrastination, of dallying and pokiness! You burn into work. It is as though gravity were removed and you walked lightly to the moon like an angel."
> *– Brenda Ueland, American author*

loquacious *(loh-KWAY-shus), adjective*
Verbose; chatty; the habit of talking nonstop.
> *Amy and Donna are each so LOQUACIOUS, their average phone call lasts ninety minutes.*

luciferous *(loo-SI-fuh-ruhs), adjective*
Providing insight or enlightenment; illuminating.
> *Blake did not find the Ivy League LUCIFEROUS, so he decided to devote his life to world travel instead.*

lucre *(LOO-ker), noun*
Monetary reward or gain.
> *"I fear the popular notion of success stands in direct opposition in all points to the real and wholesome success. One adores public opinion, the other, private opinion; one, fame, the other, desert; one, feats, the other, humility; one, LUCRE, the other, love." – Ralph Waldo Emerson, American poet, essayist, and transcendentalist*

Luddite *(LUHD-eyt), noun*
A person who refuses to use or embrace modern technology.
> *We would not stop calling Annabel a LUDDITE until she finally got herself a Vertu cell phone like the rest of us.*

lugubrious *(loo-GOO-bree-us), adjective*
Pessimistic, emotionally downtrodden, spiritually low, sad, or depressed.
> *Prozac failed to ameliorate the patient's LUGUBRIOUS outlook on life.*

lumerpa *(loo-MER-pa), noun*
A mythological radiant bird from Asia that shines so brightly it absorbs its own shadow.
> *The presence of numerous Waterford crystal chandeliers made the ballroom shine like a LUMERPA.*

luminary *(LOO-muh-nair-ee), noun*
A person recognized as an inspirational leader in his or her field.
> *Frederick's father is a LUMINARY in the field of circumventing most income tax.*

lumpenproletariat *(LUM-pen-pro-lih-tear-ee-ut), noun*
Term used by Karl Marx to describe uneducated common people.
  It's difficult to pretend to be a member of the LUMPENPROLETARIAT when your car costs more than your next-door neighbor's house.

lustration *(luh-STRAY-shun), noun*
Purification through symbolic or ceremonial means or remembrances.
  After Melanie spent six months working with charities in third-world countries, we put her through LUSTRATION by reintroducing her to our favorite luxury boutiques.

lyceum *(LIE-see-um), noun*
A school or other place of learning.

"[Television] should be our **LYCEUM**, our Chautauqua, our Minsky's, and our Camelot." – *E. B. White, American author*

"The man who is in the MELEE knows what blows are being struck and what blood is being drawn."

———

Woodrow Wilson

Machiavellian *(mack-ee-uh-VEL-ee-uhn), adjective*
A somewhat unscrupulous and self-centered individual who is always looking out for his or her own good.
We can hardly be called MACHIAVELLIAN simply because we do what we need to do to hold on to the luxurious lifestyle to which we have become accustomed.

maelstrom *(MAIL-struhm), noun*
A situation marked by violence, turbulence, and uncertainty.
Many families who lost their fortunes during the MAELSTROM of the 1929 stock market crash are still trying to regain their social status today.

Magna Carta *(MAG-nah-KAR-tah), noun*
Any constitution that guarantees rights and liberties.
The club's charter is a MAGNA CARTA that will ensure we are able to keep our tennis courts and swimming pools open only to our most significant social contacts.

magnanimous *(mag-NAN-ih-mus), adjective*
A kind and generous act.
"In a serious struggle there is no worse cruelty than to be MAGNANIMOUS at an inopportune time." – Leon Trotsky, Bolshevik revolutionary and Marxist theorist

magnate *(MAG-nayt), noun*
A wealthy and prosperous business leader; a tycoon.
Oil MAGNATE T. Boone Pickens is now investing in wind power.

magniloquent *(mag-NILL-uh-kwuhnt), adjective*
Pompous, bombastic, and boastful.
The nouveau riche try to atone for their lack of polish with MAGNILOQUENT speech, but the result is ludicrous.

magnum *(MAG-num), noun*
An extra-large wine bottle twice the size of a regular wine bottle; a powerful handgun firing large bullets.
We doubted the taste of the event planner when we saw that the tables were filled with distasteful MAGNUMS of wines of questionable vintage.

malapropism *(MAL-ah-prop-ism), noun*
Deliberate misuse of a word or mangling of the English language, often done for comic effect.

Since Emily refused to take elocution lessons like the rest of us, her speech is constantly marred by ridiculous MALAPROPISMS.

maleficence *(muh-LEF-ih-sense), noun*
To act in a way that deliberately causes harm; behavior driven by evil intentions.
Our upstairs maid's various acts of MALEFICENCE finally caused her to be released from our family's employment.

malfeasance *(mal-FEE-zinss), noun*
Misbehavior; wrongdoing; illegal, unethical, or immoral conduct.
Gavin insists that insider trading is not MALFEASANCE; it's merely making good use of all available information.

malleable *(MAL-yah-bull), adjective*
Easily molded into different shapes; easily influenced to change one's opinion or actions.

> "I did not know that mankind was suffering for want of gold. I have seen a little of it. I know that it is very **MALLEABLE**, but not so **MALLEABLE** as wit." – *Henry David Thoreau, American author and transcendentalist*

manifest destiny *(MAN-ih-fest-DESS-tin-ee), noun*
Expansion into foreign lands, justified as being necessary or benevolent.
"It's not greed and ambition that makes wars—it's goodness. Wars are always fought for the best of reasons, for liberation or MANIFEST DES-TINY, always against tyranny and always in the best interests of human-ity." – James Garner in The Americanization of Emily

marginalize *(MAR-jin-ul-eyes), verb*
To dismiss something as less important than it actually is.
Francine has too many connections for us to snub her completely, but we have done our best to MARGINALIZE her influence.

marshal *(MAR-shul), verb*
To gather all the resources at one's disposal to achieve a goal.
Patricia MARSHALED all of her social contacts to try to get a front-row ticket for fashion week.

marsupial *(mar-SOUP-ee-uhl)*, noun
A mammal who carries its young with her after its birth in a pouch on the outside of her body, where the baby continues to develop.
> *The kangaroo is the best-known MARSUPIAL, but wombats also carry their babies in a pouch.*

marzipan *(MAR-zih-pan)*, noun
A sweet confection made of almond paste, sugar, and egg white, used as a filling in candy or as icing for cake.

> "American Danish can be doughy, heavy, sticky, tasting of prunes and is usually wrapped in cellophane. Danish Danish is light, crisp, buttery and often tastes of **MARZIPAN** or raisins; it is seldom wrapped in anything but loving care." – *R. W. Apple, Jr., American food critic*

masticate *(MAS-tih-kate)*, verb
To chew, especially to chew thoroughly.
> *The best way to appreciate the gustatory arts is to MASTICATE your personal chef's creations at as relaxed a pace as possible.*

maudlin *(MAWD-lin)*, adjective
Foolishly and mawkishly sentimental or emotional.
> *"It is a MAUDLIN and indecent verity that comes out through the strength of wine." – Joseph Conrad, Polish-born English novelist*

maunder *(MAWN-dehr)*, verb
To move, speak, or act in a random, meaningless manner.
> *Ricardo's speech MAUNDERS so much that you'd never know he was heir to one of Central America's largest fortunes.*

maverick *(MAH-ver-ik)*, noun
An unorthodox or unconventional person who does what it takes to get things done.
> *"The rugged individualist is too often mistaken for the misfit, the MAVERICK, the spoilsport, the sore thumb." – Lewis H. Lapham, former editor of* Harper's Magazine

mawkish *(MAW-kish)*, adjective
Nauseating and sickly sentimental.
> *"I would jump down Etna for any public good—but I hate a MAWKISH popularity." – John Keats, English Romantic poet*

mean *(MEEN), noun*

In arithmetic, the average value of a series of numbers, determined by taking the sum of a series and dividing by the number of items in the series.

The MEAN of the Bakersfields' fortune is nowhere near that of ours, but we tolerate the family anyway because several members are excellent golfers.

meander *(MEE-ahn-duhr), verb*

To wander aimlessly.

We fired that particular servant because he MEANDERED far too slowly from task to task.

median *(MEE-dee-en), noun*

In arithmetic, the middle number in a series of numbers arranged in order from smallest to largest.

When philanthropists Brock, Cliff, and Edward were honored at a luncheon, Cliff was called upon to speak second as his donation was the MEDIAN of the three.

melanin *(MEL-uh-nin), noun*

The pigment that determines the color of one's hair, eyes, and skin.

Tamara is unwilling to accept that, no matter how much time she spends on the sunny beaches of the Mediterranean, she will not achieve her desired tan due to her lack of MELANIN.

melee *(MAY-lay), noun*

A confused struggle involving many people.

"The man who is in the MELEE knows what blows are being struck and what blood is being drawn." – Woodrow Wilson

meliorism *(mel-ee-OR-iz-um), noun*

A philosophy of optimism that says the world is gradually improving through divine intervention or human effort—or both.

Thomas Hardy's philosophy was distinctly MELIORIST because he believed ultimately in the goodness of humankind.

mellifluous *(meh-LIH-flu-us), adjective*

Music, speech, or other sound that is sweet and pleasant to listen to.

The MELLIFLUOUS tones of his voice brought Martin many high-paying gigs for voice-overs.

mendacity *(Men-DAH-sit-tee), noun*
A tendency toward or habit of being a dishonest person.
> *"The human condition is composed of unequal parts of courage, friendship, ethics, self-sacrifice, brutality, degeneracy, and MENDACITY."*
> *– Harlan Ellison, American author*

mendicant *(MEN-dih-kant), adjective*
A monk who does not own property or, more broadly, anyone who asks for alms and begs to support himself.
> *"The woman who does her job for society inside the four walls of her home must not be considered by her husband or anyone else an economic 'dependent,' reaching out her hands in MENDICANT fashion for financial help." – Mary Gilson, American economist*

mentat *(MEN-tat), noun*
A human being capable of performing mental tasks with the accuracy and speed of a computer.
> *Our accountant is a veritable MENTAT! Did you see how fast he determined all of our charitable deductions!*

mercurial *(mer-KYOOR-ee-uhl), adjective*
Volatile, fickle, and erratic.
> *Men always tolerate Natasha's MERCURIAL nature due to her beauty and her family's great fortune.*

meretricious *(mer-i-TRISH-us), adjective*
Anything done to attract attention in an unseemly or inappropriate fashion.
> *His favorite brand of beer used MERETRICIOUS ads—TV commercials showing scantily clad young women—to attract more attention.*

meridian *(mer-ID-ee-en), noun*
Any line that runs from north to south on a map or globe.
> *He sailed his yacht straight along a MERIDIAN to the Arctic Circle.*

meritocracy *(mer-ih-TOK-ruh-see), noun*
Government or leadership by people having great merit, rather than by people with great wealth.
> *Corporate leadership in a family-owned business is determined by nepotism, not MERITOCRACY.*

meritorious *(mair-uh-TORE-ee-uhss), adjective*
Worthy of praise or reward.

> "Arrogance on the part of the **MERITORIOUS** is even more offensive to us than the arrogance of those without merit: for merit itself is offensive." – *Friedrich Nietzsche, nineteenth-century German philosopher*

metachromasis *(meh-tah-CROWM-ah-sis), noun*
The phenomenon of different substances becoming different colors and shades when stained by the same dye.

An identical cotton blend was used in the entire lot of shirts to avoid METACHROMASIS ruining the color.

metaphor *(MEH-tah-for), noun*
A sentence or phrase in which a word ordinarily associated with one thing is applied to something else, to indicate that in some way they are similar.

"If we are a METAPHOR of the universe, the human couple is the metaphor par excellence, the point of intersection of all forces and the seed of all forms." – Octavio Paz Lozano, Mexican writer, poet, and diplomat

metaphysics *(met-a-FIZ-iks), noun*
The study of arguments, thoughts, and principles based primarily on thinking and abstract reasoning rather than hard facts that can be demonstrated through physical evidence.

"During my METAPHYSICS final, I cheated by looking into the soul of the person sitting next to me." – Woody Allen, American film director, writer, and comedian

metastasize *(meh-TA-sti-size), verb*
The tendency of cancer cells to spread from a tumor throughout the body.

Byron's ugly nature quickly METASTASIZED in our group, as he spread lies and gossip among more and more of our social contacts.

metallism *(MEH-tah-liz-um), noun*
The belief that money must either be made of precious metal or backed by precious metal held in reserve—usually gold or silver.

Richard Nixon abolished the gold standard for U.S. currency, and METALLISM declined as a result.

mete *(MEET), verb*
To distribute or allot.
> *After Elyssia ran up several of her father's platinum cards, he METED out substantial punishment for her by not allowing her to shop at exclusive boutiques for an entire week.*

meticulous *(meh-TICK-yuh-luhss), adjective*
Extremely precise; fussy.
> *The overly METICULOUS maître d' made us self-conscious and detracted from our enjoyment of the meal.*

métier *(MAY-tee-yay), noun*
One's occupation, profession, field of work, etc.
> *Since her family started one of Wall Street's most profitable houses, it's only natural that Ellen's MÉTIER would be finance.*

miasma *(my-AZ-mah), noun*
An unhealthy atmosphere or environment; an unpleasant feeling pervading the air.

> "These appearances, which bewilder you, are merely electrical phenomena not uncommon—or it may be there they have their ghastly origin in the rank **MIASMA** of the tarn" – *Edgar Allan Poe, American author and poet*

microcosm *(my-kruh-KAHZ-uhm), noun*
A representation of something on a very small scale.
> *"Each particle is a MICROCOSM, and faithfully renders the likeness of the world." – Ralph Waldo Emerson, American poet, essayist, and transcendentalist*

mien *(MEEN), noun*
A person's look or manner.
> *Dan's country-bumpkin MIEN effectively hides his shrewd business tactics.*

milieu *(mill-YOU), noun*
Surroundings, especially surroundings of a social or cultural nature.
> *Poetry readings and coffee shops are not Andrew's MILIEU of choice.*

millenarianism *(mil-uh-NAIR-ee-uhn-ism))*, *noun*
Any apocalyptic religious, philosophical, or social movement that predicts radical disaster, particularly at the end of the current millenium or the beginning of the new one.

> *As they worried about the impact of computer errors on the family fortune during the change from 1999 to 2000, the Cadburys briefly believed in MILLENARIANISM.*

millenium *(mil-EN-ee-um)*, *noun*
A period of a thousand years.

> *Millicent takes a MILLENIUM to get ready for society balls, but the results, typically, are worth the wait.*

minimalism *(MIN-ih-mull-iz-um)*, *noun*
A school of art in which "less is more"—clean and uncluttered paintings; sculpture with simple lines; fiction written in a lean and spare style; and music with uncomplicated scores and minimal instruments.

> *John Cage's MINIMALIST composition 4'33" consists of four and a half minutes of silence.*

minion *(MIN-yuhn)*, *noun*
A follower of someone in an important position.

> *"I caught this morning morning's MINION, king- / dom of daylight's dauphin, dapple-dawn-drawn Falcon, in his riding." – Gerard Manley Hopkins, English poet and Jesuit priest*

minutiae *(mih-NOO-shuh)*, *noun*
Small, trifling matters that one encounters on an average day.

> *The MINUTIAE of golf, tennis, and spa treatments at the club can become utterly tiresome.*

misanthrope *(MISS-anne-throwp)*, *noun*
A person of anti-social nature who dislikes other people and thinks poorly of them until they give him reason not to.

> *Harold has become a veritable MISANTHROPE since Anabelle refused to attend the regatta with him.*

misconstrue *(miss-kuhn-STROO)*, *verb*
To misinterpret or to take in a wrong sense.

> *The disagreement over the price of the yacht was due merely to the fact that David MISCONSTRUED the terms of the offer.*

misogyny *(mih-SAHJ-uh-nee), noun*
An intense hatred of women.

A lifetime of rejection had transformed him from a loving person into a rabid MISOGYNIST.

missive *(MISS-iv), noun*
An official or formal letter.

He sent out a MISSIVE informing all employees that, henceforth, there would be no smoking in their quarters—but he forgot to remove the ashtrays.

mnemonic *(neh-MON-ik), adjective, noun*
A rhyme, sentence, or other word pattern designed to help one memorize facts.

Roy G. Biv is the MNEMONIC for the colors of a rainbow: red, orange, yellow, green, blue, indigo, violet.

modernism *(MOD-er-nih-zum), noun*
Describes a modern avant-garde style of painting, sculpture, or architecture.

"Post-modernism is MODERNISM with the optimism taken out." – Robert Hewison, British historian

modicum *(MOD-ih-kuhm), noun*
A modest amount; a small quantity.

> "To be human is to have one's little **MODICUM** of romance secreted away in one's composition." – *Mark Twain*

moiety *(MOY-ih-tee), noun*
A part, portion, or share.

When I go out to dinner with my wife and kids, I don't order a meal for myself, as my dinner is a MOIETY from each of theirs.

monastic *(moh-NAS-tik), adjective*
Relating to the practice of withdrawing from society to live a quiet, contemplative life, often dedicated to religious faith.

Saint Pachomius founded the first organized Christian MONASTIC community.

monistic *(moh-NIS-tik)*, *noun*
The idea that everything—including philosophy, religion, and mysticism—can be reduced to a single substance or explained by a single principle.
Of course we believe the world is MONISTIC. Wealth is the source of everything in the universe.

monotheism *(MOH-no-THEE-iz-um)*, *noun*
A belief in one omnipotent, omniscient God who is actively involved in the workings of both the physical universe that He created and the society of men who dwell in it.
Christianity, Judaism, and Islam are all MONOTHEISTIC.

moot *(MOOT)*, *adjective*
A fact or point that is uncertain or no longer relevant.
Whether to continue injecting growth hormones became a MOOT point as Alex grew from five feet to five-nine in eighteen months.

morass *(muh-RASS)*, *noun*
A confusing or troublesome situation from which it is difficult to disentangle oneself.
"One idea is enough to organize a life and project it / Into unusual but viable forms, but many ideas merely / Lead one thither into a MORASS of their own good intentions." – John Ashbery, American poet

mordantly *(MORE-dant-lee)*, *adverb*
To behave in a negative, malicious, or damaging fashion.
"The ocean looked dead too, dead gray waves hissing MORDANTLY along the beach." – John Fowles, British novelist and essayist

mores *(MORE-ayz)*, *noun*
The accepted norms of social behavior for the time and society in which you live.
Grant learned the hard way that MORES vary from country to country when he made the faux pas of trying to shake the hand of the Thai businessman.

moribund *(MOR-ih-bund)*, *adjective*
Lacking vigor; soon to be dead or defunct.
Ever since its head chef left for the Food Network, that gourmet restaurant has become MORIBUND and is likely to close soon.

morose *(muh-ROHSS), adjective*
Gloomy and ill-humored.
> *Now that his parents have taken away his private plane, Anthony has become positively MOROSE.*

M

motif *(mow-TEEF), noun*
A dominant or frequently repeated theme, design, image, or idea.
> *The Whittingtons' china has a diamond-shaped MOTIF that is a testament to how the family made its fortune.*

mot juste *(MOW-zshoost), noun*
The perfect word or phrase to communicate precisely what you mean to say.
> *Years of elocution lessons have left Paulina capable of leavening every occasion with a suitable MOT JUSTE.*

multifarious *(mull-tea-FAH-ree-us), adjective*
Varied, wide-ranging, versatile, covering many different areas or fields.
> *Yvonne's MULTIFARIOUS talents include showing horses, lacrosse, and opera singing.*

multilateral *(mull-tea-LAH-terr-ul), adjective*
An agreement or accord requiring two nations or states to take the same position or action on an issue or problem.
> *A pacifist, he frequently spoke out for MULTILATERAL nuclear disarmament.*

munificent *(myoo-NIFF-uh-suhnt), adjective*
Characterized by great generosity.
> *The Pattersons are so MUNIFICENT that they give to charity year-round rather than merely at times when giving offers tax benefits.*

muse *(MEWS), noun*
The source of one's creative or artistic inspiration, named after the mythical Greek *Muses* said to be patrons of the fine arts.
> *"O for a MUSE of fire, that would ascend / The brightest heaven of invention." – William Shakespeare*

mutable *(MYOO-tuh-bull), adjective*
Subject to change at a moment's notice.

> "For is the same! For, be it joy or sorrow, / The path of its departure still is free: / Man's yesterday may ne'er be like his morrow; / Nought may endure but **MUTABILITY**" – *Percy Bysshe Shelley, English Romantic poet*

myriad *(MIR-ee-ud), noun*
An abundance of possibilities, selections, choices, or options.
The MYRIAD possibilities inherent in selling her ex-husband's family diamonds for $10 million boggled Elizabeth's mind.

"The comic spirit is given to us in order that we may analyze, weigh, and clarify things in us which NETTLE us, or which we are outgrowing, or trying to reshape."

———

Thornton Wilder, American playwright and novelist

nacelle *(NAY-sell), noun*

The pod-shaped outer hull of an airplane engine.

> *Bentley always has his family crest imprinted on the NACELLE of each of his private planes.*

nadir *(NAY-der), noun*

Rock-bottom, the lowest of the low, the worst a thing can get or become.

> *We always have to attend the Wallingtons' Christmas party, due to their standing, but, in truth, that dreadfully boring event is always the NADIR of our social calendar.*

nanosecond *(NAN-oh-sek-uhnd), noun*

A time period equal to one billionth of a second.

> *Amanda's new diamond-encrusted watch not only has a second hand but also a NANOSECOND hand.*

nascent *(NAY-sent), adjective*

Having just been born or invented and still in the early stages of growth and development.

> *It's always amusing to watch the nouveau riche during the NASCENT period of their adjustment to luxury.*

nationalism *(NAH-shin-ul-iz-um), noun*

The idea that citizens should take great pride in their country and support it to the hilt; extreme patriotism.

> *Albert Einstein called NATIONALISM "the measles of mankind."*

natter *(NAH-ter), verb*

To talk ceaselessly; babble.

> *The way Emily NATTERS endlessly about her family's new yacht is revolting to those of us who have owned several yachts over the years.*

Nebuchadnezzar *(neb-yoo-could-NEZ-er), noun*

A king mentioned in the Old Testament of the Bible who destroyed Jerusalem and exiled the Israelites to Babylonia.

> *"And NEBUCHADNEZZAR was driven from men, and did eat grass as oxen, and his body was wet with the dew of heaven, till his hairs were grown like eagles' feathers, and his nails like birds' claws." – Daniel 4:33*

nebulous *(NEB-yoo-luhs), adjective*

An idea or plan that is vague and not well thought out; ill-defined; lacking concretes.

Jay's plans for what he would do when he graduated college were NEBU-LOUS at best.

necessitate *(nuh-SESS-ih-tate), verb*
To make necessary; to obligate.
> *"Each coming together of man and wife, even if they have been mated for many years, should be a fresh adventure; each winning should NECESSITATE a fresh wooing." – Marie Carmichael Stopes, British scientist and birth-control pioneer*

necromancy *(NEH-kroh-man-see), noun*
The ability to gain new knowledge by communicating with the dead; magic and trickery in general.
> *"The so-called science of poll-taking is not a science at all but mere NECROMANCY." – E. B. White, American author*

nefarious *(nih-FARE-ee-us), adjective*
Inherently evil, malicious, and unjust.
> *"You were preceded by your NEFARIOUS reputation," the sheriff said to the gunslinger who had just sidled up to the bar.*

nemesis *(nem-UH-sis), noun*
An opponent one is unable to defeat.

> "How wonderful to live with one's **NEMESIS**! You may be miserable, but you feel forever in the right." – *Erica Jong, American author and teacher*

neoconservative *(NEE-oh-kon-SERVE-ah-tive), noun*
A liberal who has become a conservative.
> *We've removed Bradley from our list of social contacts because he has become such a NEOCONSERVATIVE.*

neologism *(nee-AHL-uh-jizm), noun*
A new word, or an "old" word used in a new way.
> *William Shakespeare coined such NEOLOGISMS as "gossip," "swagger," and "domineering."*

neonatal *(NEE-oh-NAY-tul), adjective*
Of, or relating to newborn children.

> *Honestly, the Atkinsons treat their grown children as though they still require NEONATAL care. No wonder they never get invited to any of our galas.*

neophyte *(NEE-uh-fight), noun*
A beginner or novice.

> "Like footmen and upstairs maids, wine stewards are portrayed as acolytes of the privileged, ever eager to intimidate the **NEOPHYTE** and spurn the unwary." – *Frank J. Prial, former* New York Times *wine columnist*

nepotism *(NEH-poh-tiz-um), noun*
The practice of a business owner or manager giving favorable treatment to his family; e.g., hiring his son for a summer job, giving the company's advertising work to his wife's ad agency, etc.

> *Rampant NEPOTISM in the company prevented most of the employees from rising very far up the ranks.*

nether *(NETH-uhr), adjective*
Located below or under something else.

> *"I know a lady in Venice would have walked barefoot to Palestine for a touch of his NETHER lip."* – *William Shakespeare*

nettle *(NET-uhl), verb*
To provoke, irritate, or annoy.

> *"The comic spirit is given to us in order that we may analyze, weigh, and clarify things in us which NETTLE us, or which we are outgrowing, or trying to reshape."* – *Thornton Wilder, American playwright and novelist*

nexus *(NEK-sus), noun*
A linkage or connection between two or more things.

> *"Every time a message seems to grab us, and we think, 'I just might try it,' we are at the NEXUS of choice and persuasion that is advertising."* – *Andrew Hacker, American media critic*

niggling *(NIG-ling), adjective*
Demanding a great deal of care, attention, or time; or, trifling and insignificant.

People just don't understand how difficult it is on us to attend to all the NIGGLING needs of our servants.

N

nihilism *(NIE-uh-lizz-uhm), noun*
The belief that nothing can be known with absolute certainty, resulting in an intense skepticism of almost everything, especially religion and moral principles.

"NIHILISM is best done by professionals." – Iggy Pop, American singer and songwriter

nimbus *(NIM-bus), noun*
A halo of light surrounding the head of a saint or other holy person.

"Sally is such a goody two-shoes, you'd think she would have a NIMBUS on top of her head," Nancy said to the girls.

nitid *(NIT-id), adjective*
Bright and lustrous.

Brock and Jenny flew through NITID moonbeams in Brock's new Gulfstream GIV personal jet.

noblesse oblige *(no-BLESS-oh-BLEEZH), noun*
An act of generosity, charity, or kindness performed by a rich person for the benefit of someone less fortunate than himself, viewed by the giver as paying the universe back for his good fortune.

Donald gave the young man a job not out of a sense of pity or guilt, but out of a sense of NOBLESSE OBLIGE.

nomenclature *(NO-men-klay-cherr), noun*
A labeling or naming system used in a specialized field or industry.

Even an activity as seemingly simple as macramé has a NOMENCLATURE all it's own, indecipherable to the layperson or newbie.

nominal *(NAHM-ih-nl), adjective*
A thing of relatively minor importance; an insignificant amount or volume of something.

For a NOMINAL fee, the store delivers your new widescreen TV to your home and sets it up for you.

nominalism *(NAHM-ih-nl-iz-um), noun*

A philosophy that denies the existence of universal truths.

> *Some scientists suspect that, rather than being universal, the laws of physics may vary in different regions of the universe—a strong supporting argument for NOMINALISM.*

nonagenarian *(none-uh-jen-AIR-ee-en), noun*

A person in his or her nineties.

> *When you're a NONAGENARIAN, it begins to occur to you that you could in fact live to be one hundred.*

non compos mentis *(NAHN-KAHM-pohs-MEN-tiss), adjective*

Crazy; insane; not in one's right mind.

> *When Bryce suggested he was considering the ministry, rather than joining the family bond business, we were certain he was NON COMPOS MENTIS.*

nondescript *(non-dih-SKRIPT), adjective*

Lacking distinction; ordinary.

> "Actors ought to be larger than life. You come across quite enough ordinary, **NONDESCRIPT** people in daily life and I don't see why you should be subjected to them on the stage too." – *Donald Sinden, British actor*

nonentity *(non-EN-tih-tee), noun*

A person or thing considered completely unimportant.

> *Ever since Cassandra scorned us at the Brackingtons' Thanksgiving gala, we have taken to treating her as a NONENTITY.*

nonpareil *(non-pah-RAYLE), adjective*

Without equal or peer.

We could tell Jeanette was a typical parvenu when she attempted to convince us that Bennington Posh Couture golf bags are NONPAREIL.

nonpartisan *(non-PAHR-tih-zuhn), adjective*

Not in support of a particular political party or special interest group.

> *The Vallinghams pride themselves in being NONPARTISAN, but they have never been known to vote even for a moderate Democrat.*

nonplussed *(none-plust), adjective*
In modern usage, not being bothered by commotion; undisturbed by what is happening around you; in traditional usage, the opposite of the modern definition.

The construction on the bridge left him NONPLUSSED, because he enjoyed listening to books on tape in his car.

non sequitur *(nahn-SEH-kwit-ur), noun*
A conclusion or statement that does not seem to follow from that which preceded it.

Hilary's belief that she was now welcome in our group was, clearly, a NON SEQUITUR on her part.

nostrum *(NAH-strum), noun*
An ineffective solution that is a quick fix or band-aid, covering up a problem or masking its symptoms, but never addressing its root cause for a permanent fix.

"America's present need is not NOSTRUMS but normalcy." – Warren G. Harding

nouveau riche *(noo-voh-REESH), adjective, noun*
A person who has recently acquired wealth.

The most distinguished families in the club snubbed him because he was NOUVEAU RICHE.

noxious *(NOCK-shuss), adjective*
Morally harmful and pernicious.

Even with his wealth, good looks, and charm, Steven has such a NOXIOUS personality that we always feel awful after spending time with him.

nuance *(NOO-ahnts), noun*
A subtle difference in meaning, expression, or tone.

"[Venice] in winter is rich with the bittersweet NUANCE and somber beauty of the once-was." – Terry Weeks, American travel writer

nubile *(NOO-bile), adjective*
Of sexually developed and attractive youth.

We have explained time and again to Melinda that she must get a personal trainer like the rest of us to be truly NUBILE.

nugatory *(NOO-guh-tore-ee), adjective*
Trifling, worthless, and ineffective.
> *We spend our time like most, with the NUGATORY pastimes of polo, tennis on grass courts, and weekends in Europe.*

nullify *(NUHL-uh-fie), verb*
To make something valueless or ineffective.
> *We keep our collections under lock and key because, sometimes, merely breathing on them NULLIFIES their value.*

nymph *(NIMF), noun*
A spirit linked to a particular place or element.

"Reason is a supple **NYMPH**, and slippery as a fish by nature." – *D. H. Lawrence, British author*

"The bottom of being is left logically OPAQUE to us, as something which we simply come upon and find, and about which (if we wish to act) we should pause and wonder as little as possible."

———

William James, American psychologist and philosopher

obdurate *(OB-doo-rit), adjective*
Stubborn and unyielding.

> "The fates are not quite **OBDURATE**; / They have a grim, sardonic way / Of granting them who supplicate / The thing they wanted yesterday."
> – *Roselle Mercier Montgomery, American poet*

obeisance *(oh-BEE-sance), noun*
Deferential respect or homage, or an act or gesture expressing the same.
Rachael practiced OBEISANCE by allowing the elderly woman to sit in her plush opera box, rather than in the mezzanine.

obfuscate *(OB-few-skate), verb*
To talk or write about a subject in a way that deliberately makes it unclear, selectively omits certain facts, or communicates wrong ideas or impressions, so that the listener or reader does not grasp the whole truth of the situation.
Despite his Ivy League education, Alexander seems able only to OBFUSCATE any subject upon which he touches.

objurgatory *(AHB-jer-ga-tor-ee), adjective*
A critical attitude voicing or implying an objection or complaint.
"I can to some extent sympathize with the OBJURGATORY tone of certain critics who feel that I write too much." – Joyce Carol Oates, American author

oblique *(oh-BLEAK), adjective*
Indirectly or deviously achieved.
If direct appeals do not work, Amanda is always quick to use OBLIQUE methods in order to get her father to buy her whatever luxury item she wants.

obsequious *(uhb-SEE-kwi-us), adjective*
Subservient; eager to listen and to please others to an excessive degree; behaving in the manner of a servant or slave.

> "[The political mind] is a strange mixture of vanity and timidity, of an **OBSEQUIOUS** attitude at one time and a delusion of grandeur at another time. – *Calvin Coolidge*

obsolescence *(ob-suh-LESS-uhnts)*, *noun*
The state of being no longer useful.

Roderick found, to his dismay, that some of the new Maserati models had lapsed into OBSOLESCENCE almost as soon as they hit the showroom floor.

obstinate *(AHB-stih-nit)*, *adjective*
Inflexible in one's opinions and attitudes; refusing to change or accede to the wishes of others.

"The male sex still constitutes in many ways the most OBSTINATE vested interest one can find." – Francis Pakenham, British social reformer

obstreperous *(ob-STREP-er-us)*, *adjective*
Describes a trouble-maker who is noisy, unruly, or otherwise attracts attention in his endeavor to be difficult.

Two OBSTREPEROUS employees made the training class a nightmare for the instructor.

obtuse *(ahb-TOOS)*, *adjective*
Lacking understanding, intelligence, and perception; unable to comprehend; having a dense mind.

Thomas was so OBTUSE, he didn't realize his inappropriate behavior was making his friends uncomfortable.

obviate *(OB-vee-ate)*, *verb*
To anticipate, and therefore prevent, difficulties or disadvantages.

We changed the location of our fall gala at the last minute, OBVIATING the need to cut anyone from our ever-expanding guest list.

occlude *(oh-KLOOD)*, *verb*
To block or obstruct; to close off a passage or entranceway.

Debris from the second-floor construction OCCLUDED the entryway to the laundry room in Linda's beach house.

occultation *(ahk-uhl-TAY-shin)*, *noun*
The act of hiding or blocking from view.

With disguises offering a bit of needed OCCULTATION, we were able to hit Manhattan's hot spots away from the glare of the dreaded paparazzi.

odal *(OH-dull), noun*
Absolute ownership of a property that is beyond dispute and can never be revoked.

> *Among the Norse, land allotted to a warrior at the time of conquest became ODAL after his family had held it for three generations.*

odious *(OH-dee-us), adjective*
To be so offensive or disgusting that people are repulsed or experience revulsion.

> *"To depend upon a profession is a less ODIOUS form of slavery than to depend upon a father." – Virginia Woolf, British essayist and novelist*

odoriferous *(oh-der-ih-ferr-us), adjective*
Bad smelling; foul.

> *Eleanor believed she would enjoy her weekend trek through the South American rainforest, but she found the animals too noisy, the constant rain unpleasant, and the forest's ODORIFEROUS vegetation distasteful.*

oeniphile *(EE-nuh-file), noun*
A connoisseur of wines.

> *Despite his relatively young age, Brad's family has brought him up to be a consummate OENIPHILE.*

oeuvre *(OO-vruh), noun*
An artist's, writer's, or composer's body of work, treated as a whole.

> *Esmerelda is familiar with and adores all of Puccini's OEUVRE, but many find his operas overly mawkish.*

offal *(OH-full), noun*
Rotting waste; decaying organic matter. In general, anything considered garbage or refuse.

> *"I have often told you that I am that little fish who swims about under a shark and, I believe, lives indelicately on its OFFAL." – Zelda Fitzgerald, American author*

officious *(oh-FISH-ee-us), adjective*
Asserting authority or power in an obnoxious, overbearing, or pompous manner.

> *"There is immunity in reading, immunity in formal society, in office routine, in the company of old friends and in the giving of OFFICIOUS help to strangers, but there is no sanctuary in one bed from the memory of another." – Cyril Connolly, British literary critic and writer*

ogle *(OH-guhl), verb*
To look at in an amorous or impertinent way.

> *No one would want to trade places with us if they only knew how tiresome it becomes to have the paparazzi constantly OGLING you.*

olfactory *(ole-FAK-tore-ee), adjective*
Related to the sense of smell.

> *Miranda and Jonathan savored the OLFACTORY pleasures wafting from early-opening bakeries on the Upper West Side.*

oligarchy *(OH-lih-gar-kee), noun*
A nation, state, or other place where the population is governed by a relatively small group of people, especially when all are members of the same family.

> *Most family owned businesses are OLIGARCHIES, not democracies.*

oligopoly *(oh-lih-GAH-poll-lee), noun*
Control of an industry, sector, or market by a small number of companies dominating that particular niche.

> *One can argue that Intel and Microsoft collectively are an OLIGOPOLY in personal computing.*

ombudsman *(ohm-BUDZ-min), noun*
A person who is charged with mediating disputes between businesses and consumers, students and a university, etc.

> *All it took to get Brock off of academic probation at U Penn was to have his father remind the OMBUDSMAN of how much money the family had donated to the university over the years.*

omnipotent *(ahm-NIP-uh-tuhnt), adjective*
All powerful.

> "An **OMNIPOTENT** God is the only being with no reason to lie." – *Mason Cooley, American author*

omniscient *(ahm-NIH-shent), adjective*
Describes someone who knows everything.

> *"The god of love, if omnipotent and OMNISCIENT, must be the god of cancer and epilepsy as well." – George Bernard Shaw, Irish playwright*

omnivore *(AHM-nih-vore), noun*
An animal that eats both plants and other animals.
> *I ordered a delicious steak salad with crumbled blue cheese—an OMNI-VORE'S delight.*

onerous *(OH-nerr-us), adjective*
Describes a difficult task or heavy responsibility that one does not desire.
> *Caring for his son's large aquarium quickly went from an interesting hobby to an ONEROUS burden.*

onomatopoeia *(on-uh-ma-tuh-PEE-uh), noun*
Words that sound like, or suggest, their meaning.
> *The spring gala, with its popping corks, fizzing champagne glasses, and thumping music was a cornucopia of ONOMATOPOEIA.*

onus *(OH-nuss), noun*
Obligation, responsibility, duty, or burden.
> *The ONUS for choosing the color scheme for our new lacrosse uniforms fell ultimately to Tabitha, who had previously chosen the design for our polo uniforms.*

opaque *(oh-PAYK), adjective*
Hard to understand; obscure.
> *"The bottom of being is left logically OPAQUE to us, as something which we simply come upon and find, and about which (if we wish to act) we should pause and wonder as little as possible." – William James, American psychologist and philosopher*

operose *(OP-uh-roass), adjective*
Hard-working and industrious.
> *What's the point of being OPEROSE when our social connections help us to achieve success with little effort?*

opprobrium *(uh-PRO-bree-uhm), noun*
Disgrace incurred by outrageously shameful conduct.
> *Natasha incurred OPPROBRIUM when, in a fit of anger, she deliberately smashed her Waterford crystal wine glass at the Smythingtons' annual Thanksgiving gala.*

opine *(oh-PYNE), verb*
To give your opinion.
> *The way that Charlotte OPINES about fashion, you'd think she created couture rather than just purchasing it.*

opulent *(AHP-yoo-lent), adjective*
Reflecting wealth and affluence.
> *Donald Trump showcases his OPULENT lifestyle by wearing designer suits, drinking Cristal champagne, and traveling in private airplanes.*

opus *(OH-puss), noun*
A major work of music written by a composer.
> *The Breckinridges commissioned the composer's next OPUS, which will be debuted at the family's fall ball.*

orator *(OR-ray-ter), noun*
A skilled and persuasive public speaker.
> *Tom over-estimated his abilities as an ORATOR and, consequently, stayed at the podium far longer than the audience wanted him to.*

ordinance *(OR-dih-nance), noun*
A specific law or regulation.
> *The lavish tree house Roger built for his kids was in clear violation of at least half a dozen local ORDINANCES.*

orgiastic *(or-jee-AS-tick), adjective*
Arousing unrestrained emotional release.
> *William becomes loathsomely ORGIASTIC when he attends and bids at art auctions.*

orotund *(OR-uh-tund), adjective*
Characterizes a voice distinguished by strength, fullness, and clearness.
> *In a beguilingly OROTUND voice, the conductor offered a synopsis of the evening's opera.*

orthodox *(OR-thuh-docks), adjective*
Mainstream; conventional; adhering to the strictest interpretation of a law or religion.
> *ORTHODOX medicine has long ignored the obvious effect diet and nutrition have on health and illness.*

oscillate *(AHSS-uh-layt), verb*
To change one's mind frequently about beliefs and opinions.
> *We can hardly keep up with Lydia's choices regarding the quality of luxury jewelers because she OSCILLATES from week to week.*

osculant *(OS-kyuh-lunt), adjective*
Describes a passionate kiss.

> *"He planted a hell of a kiss on me: lips, tongue, the entire OSCULANT assemblage."* – *Charlaine Harris,* New York Times *bestselling mystery writer*

osmosis *(oz-MOW-sis), noun*
A subtle and gradual assimilation of new knowledge based on one's proximity to another with greater knowledge.

> *Just hanging out with Bob, who was an A student, seemed to help Vincent improve his grades, as if he was learning what Bob knew through OSMOSIS.*

ostensibly *(ah-STEN-sih-blee), adverb*
Something that exists or has been done for what would seem an obvious reason.

> *The nouveau riche always seek to spend time with us, OSTENSIBLY to be absorbed into our world, but they will never fully be a part of our community.*

ostentatious *(ah-sten-TAY-shus), adjective*
Pretentious; presented in a showy manner so as to impress others; visibly flaunting one's wealth or success.

> *"The man who is OSTENTATIOUS of his modesty is twin to the statue that wears a fig-leaf."* – *Mark Twain*

ostracize *(OS-truh-size), verb*
To exclude from society, friendship, community, etc.

> *Once we learned that Sasha had been planting stories about us in the society pages, we, of course, had to OSTRACIZE her permanently from our group.*

outré *(oo-TRAY), adjective*
Radically unconventional; outside the limits of expected conduct or behavior.

> *"One of life's intriguing paradoxes is that hierarchical social order makes cheap rents and OUTRÉ artists' colonies possible."* – *Florence King, American author*

overweening *(OH-ver-WEE-ning), adjective*
Extremely presumptuous, arrogant, and overconfident.

> "Golf is an open exhibition of **OVERWEENING** ambition, courage deflated by stupidity, skill soured by a whiff of arrogance." – *Alistair Cooke, British-born American journalist and broadcaster*

oxidation *(oks-ih-DAY-shin), noun*
A chemical reaction that increases the oxygen content of a compound or material.

When Carlton viewed the wreck of the Titanic from the window of a submersible, he was shocked to see how OXIDATION had ravaged the ship.

oxymoron *(ok-see-MORE-on), noun*
A phrase made by combining two words that are contradictory or incongruous.

Melissa sheepishly used the OXYMORON "accidentally on purpose" to explain to her father why her emergency credit card included a charge for $500 Manolo Blahnik heels.

"*I want to kiss God on His nose and watch Him sneeze / and so do you. / Not out of disrespect. / Out of PIQUE. / Out of a man-to-man thing.*"

———

Anne Sexton, American poet and author

P

palaver *(pa-LAH-ver), noun*
A rambling, meandering stream-of-consciousness conversation spoken to prove or make a point.
> *Don't ask Eileen about collecting art. The result will be twenty minutes of mind-numbing PALAVER.*

palimpsest *(PAL-imp-sest), noun*
A parchment manuscript on which the text is written over older, earlier text, much like an oil portrait or landscape painted over another painting.
> *The newest addition to the Pattersons' rare manuscript collection turned out to be a PALIMPSEST, covering a text nearly 1,000 years old.*

palindrome *(pal-in-DROHM), noun*
A word or sentence that reads the same forwards as backwards.
> *At private school, Evelyn learned about PALINDROMES, including, "Madam, I'm Adam."*

palliate *(PAL-ee-ate), verb*
To treat a patient so that his symptoms abate even though he still has the disease.
> *We introduced Amanda to Roberto, in attempt to PALLIATE the broken heart that Amanda suffered over her breakup with one of the scions of the Chesterfield family.*

pallid *(PAL-id), adjective*
A wan, sickly, washed-out appearance indicating illness or weakness, or lack of energy, strength, and vitality.
> *Many of us maintain a PALLID pallor because we want to make it clear that we do not need to go outdoors unless we so choose.*

palpable *(PAL-pah-bull), adjective*
Refers to something so strong or intense that its presence is impossible to ignore.
> *When Alistair did not give Lorissa the luxury watch she was expecting for her birthday, the silence was PALPABLE.*

panacea *(pan-uh-SEE-uh), noun*
A universal solution for all problems, diseases, or woes.
> *Parents today see buying their kids everything they want as a PANACEA for misery, boredom, and unhappiness.*

pandemic *(pan-DEM-ik), noun*
An outbreak of a disease that threatens to spread rapidly and endanger the population of an entire nation or planet.
> *Many scientists feared that Asian bird flu would become a pandemic.*

Pangaea *(pan-GEE-uh), noun*
A single massive continent that comprised all the land on the Earth before the crust shifted and the *Pangaea* divided into many smaller continents.
> *The PANGAEA existed until Mesozoic times, when it divided into two separate continents.*

panoply *(PAN-oh-plee), noun*
A complete or impressive collection; a splendid or abundant array.
> *The gallery offered a PANOPLY of African face masks.*

pantheon *(PAN-thee-on), noun*
The group of all the gods of a particular religion or culture, or a group of important people in a particular field or region.
> *The sons of Odin, Thor and Loki, represent good and evil in the PAN-THEON of the Norse gods.*

paradigm *(PAH-ruh-dyme), noun*
An observation or discovery in conflict with known facts, beliefs, and theories.
> *The new PARADIGM for fashion, according to Sasha, is extremely expensive clothes that look as inexpensive as possible.*

paradox *(PAIR-uh-doks), noun*
A seemingly absurd and self-contradicting situation that seems impossible but may in fact be true.
> *The article profiled a man who was a real PARADOX; he was grossly overweight, yet had tremendous athletic stamina.*

parameter *(pah-RAM-ih-terr), noun*
A factor or variable that must be taken into account when solving a problem or understanding a situation.
> *The weight of Paul's grand piano is a PARAMETER that must be taken into account when building the mansion's new music room and ballroom.*

parity *(PAH-rih-tee), noun*
The condition of everyone being more or less equal.
> *The firemen received a raise to help them achieve pay PARITY with the sanitation workers and police department.*

parlance *(PAR-lunss), noun*
To speak in the vernacular or jargon used by a particular industry, profession, or group.
> *By using the terms "discourse," "pedagogy," and "literary criticism," the professors spoke in the PARLANCE of academia.*

parsimonious *(par-sih-MOAN-ee-us), adjective*
To be conservative in spending and tight with a dollar; to agree to part with money or other resources only grudgingly and after much cajoling.
> *Esmerelda can be surprisingly PARSIMONIOUS, considering that her family's fortune is among the greatest possessed by our social contacts.*

pathological *(path-a-LODGE-ick-uhl), adjective*
Compulsive in nature; possessing of a belief system or mindset that makes one unable to resist repetition of a particular type of behavior, e.g., a *pathological* liar.
> *Diane's PATHOLOGICAL need for attention has caused her, on more than one occasion, to plant lies about herself in the society pages.*

paucity *(PAW-city), noun*
A lack of something, a small supply or limited selection.
> *"It is very strange, and very melancholy, that the PAUCITY of human pleasures should persuade us ever to call hunting one of them." – Samuel Johnson, British moralist and poet*

pecuniary *(pih-KYOO-nee-air-ee), adjective*
Something related to money.
> *Because all of Craig's articles had a strong PECUNIARY slant, his editor moved him from the features page to the finance page.*

pedagogue *(PED-ah-gog), noun*
A strict, humorless, no-nonsense teacher.
> *"The negative cautions of science are never popular. If the experimentalist would not commit himself, the social philosopher, the preacher, and the PEDAGOGUE tried the harder to give a short-cut answer." – Margaret Mead, American cultural anthropologist*

pedantry *(PEH-dan-tree), noun*
An obsessive behavior of being proper and technically correct down to the last detail.

> *Samuel Taylor Coleridge defined PEDANTRY as "the use of words unsuitable to the time, place, and company."*

pejorative *(pih-JOR-a-tiv), adjective*
Insulting; meant as a put-down or to belittle the other person.

> *"Wordsmith" is a corporate term used to denote someone who is a good writer, but professional writers see it as PEJORATIVE.*

penitent *(PEN-ih-tent), adjective*
Feeling sorry and regretful that you have done something wrong.

> *According to Ambrose Bierce's jaded view, the PENITENT are typically those undergoing or awaiting punishment.*

penultimate *(pen-UHL-tah-met), adjective*
Next to last in importance.

> *The Whittingtons' Christmas gala is the PENULTIMATE party of the social season.*

per capita *(per-KA-pih-tah), adjective*
Per person; pertaining to a single individual.

> *We find it satisfying to mull over the fact that the PER CAPITA income among our social contacts is greater than that of many countries.*

perfervid *(per-FUR-vid), adjective*
Overly intense and passionate; overblown and dramatic.

> *We laughed at the distastefully PERFERVID love letters that Roland sent to Germaine.*

perfunctory *(per-FUNK-ter-ee), adjective*
Implemented or executed quickly, without much care or thought put into it.

> *"The tale is so contrived and PERFUNCTORY that many readers will be tempted to skip to the real story in the second half of the book." – Tim Parks, British novelist*

peripatetic *(per-ih-pa-TET-ik), adjective*
Someone who wanders from career to career, job to job, company to company, or place to place, seemingly without a clear goal or definiteness of purpose.

> *While waiting to receive his trust fund at age thirty, Giles lived a PERIPATETIC lifestyle.*

periphery *(puh-RIFF-uh-ree), noun*
The outermost part or boundary; the outside edge.
Craig's plans are always on the PERIPHERY of what could charitably be called normal behavior.

permeate *(PUR-mee-ayt), verb*
To penetrate; to spread throughout.
The scent of Donna's exclusive perfume quickly PERMEATED the entrance hall of the Blakelys' stately home.

pernicious *(purr-NISH-us), adjective*
Resulting in damage or harm; having a debilitating effect.
We believe that, once the producers of luxury items become publicly traded companies, the results will be PERNICIOUS.

perturbation *(purr-ter-BAY-shun), noun*
Originally used to describe the phenomenon of one planet's gravitational field throwing another planet's orbit slightly out of kilter. Today, *perturbation* refers more generally to any disturbance that alters the normal state or function of a system, moving object, person, or process.

> "O polished **PERTURBATION**! golden care! / That keep'st the ports of slumber open wide / To many a watchful night." – *William Shakespeare*

petulant *(PET-chew-lant), adjective*
Describes someone who sulks, complains, or whines because he or she is acting immaturely or is ill-tempered.
Emma was sick and tired of her husband's PETULANT pouting.

phalanx *(FAY-lanks), noun*
A large division or group of soldiers grouped closely together in an orderly fashion for marching or fighting.
Philip of Macedon armed each man with a long spear so the PHALANX bristled like a porcupine.

Pharisee *(FAH-ree-see), noun*
A person who is self-righteous and hypocritical.
The state Attorney General was a PHARISEE who prosecuted others for the same crimes he was secretly committing himself.

philanthropist *(fill-ANN-throw-pist), noun*
A person who generously gives his or her time, energy, and money to charity.

> *Bill Gates is the most proactive PHILANTHROPIST out of all the billionaires who care to invest their time in contributing to charitable causes.*

philistine *(FILL-ih-steen), noun*
A crude and ignorant person who is disinterested in and does not appreciate culture and the arts.

> *"A PHILISTINE is a full-grown person whose interests are of a material and commonplace nature, and whose mentality is formed of the stock ideas and conventional ideals of his or her group and time." – Vladimir Nabokov, Russian-American novelist*

phoenix *(FEE-niks), noun*
A mythical bird about the size of an eagle, but with brilliantly colored plumage, that dies by fire and then is reborn from the ashes.

> *One day the PHOENIX appeared in the forests of France, and legend has it that all the other birds became instantly jealous.*

pied-a-terre *(pyed-ah-TARE), noun*
A second home or apartment, usually small, used as a place to stay for short trips to the location in lieu of renting a hotel room.

> *We were amazed that Alison and her family could survive in a PIED-A-TERRE containing just 2,500 square feet.*

piety *(PIE-eh-tee), noun*
Devoutly religious behavior, especially when exhibited publicly to let others know how pious you are.

> *"The path of true PIETY is so plain as to require but little political direction." – George Washington*

pique *(PEEK), noun, verb*
To generate interest or curiosity; a feeling of annoyance resulting from a perceived insult or injustice.

> *"I want to kiss God on His nose and watch Him sneeze / and so do you. / Not out of disrespect. / Out of PIQUE. / Out of a man-to-man thing." – Anne Sexton, American poet and author*

plethora *(PLETH-uh-ruh), noun*
An excessive amount of something.

Agnes tried a PLETHORA of wines before she finally decided on her favorite vintage.

pluralism *(PLOOR-al-iz-im), noun*
The understanding and tolerance of a diversity of differing cultures and views within a single society.
As long as someone comes from a family of high-standing, we wholeheartedly embrace PLURALISM.

polemic *(pah-LEM-ik), noun*
A long, rambling speech or diatribe, the goal of which is to prove a point or sway the listener to see your point of view.
"He had a strong will and a talent for POLEMIC." – Saul Bellow, American author

polymath *(POHL-ee-math), noun*
A person with a wide range of intellectual interests or a broad base of knowledge in many different disciplines.
"I had a terrible vision: I saw an encyclopedia walk up to a POLYMATH and open him up." – Karl Kraus, Austrian writer

polyphonic *(pahl-ee-FAHN-ik), adjective*
Having many different sounds.
"The guitar is a small orchestra. It is POLYPHONIC. Every string is a different color, a different voice." – Andres Segovia, Spanish classical guitarist

populism *(POP-you-liz-um), noun*
A political movement or policy that appeals to the masses—the average working man or woman—not the upper class.

"Being naked approaches being revolutionary; going barefoot is mere **POPULISM.**" *– John Updike, American novelist and literary critic*

portent *(poor-TENT), noun*
A warning sign that something bad is going to happen.
In Ray Bradbury's novel Something Wicked This Way Comes, *the carnival coming to town is a PORTENT of evil things to come.*

posit *(PAHZ-it), verb*
To suggest or propose a theory or explanation, especially one that represents new, unusual, or non-obvious thinking and conclusions.

Astronomers POSIT that Jupiter may sustain life in its clouds.

postulate *(PA-stew-late), verb*
To arrive at a theory, belief, hypothesis, or principle based upon an analysis of known facts.

"The primacy of human personality has been a POSTULATE both of Christianity and of liberal democracy." – Julian Huxley, English evolutionary biologist

potentate *(POH-ten-tayt), noun*
A powerful dictator, king, leader, or ruler.

A much-feared POTENTATE, Victor Von Doom ruled Latvia with an iron fist.

pragmatism *(PRAG-muh-tiz-um), noun*
The belief that one's actions should be guided primarily based on knowledge or opinion of what is likely to work best in a given situation; the imperative to always do what is practical and effective.

Our families have succeeded in amassing great wealth over many generations because we are all, at heart, practitioners of PRAGMATISM.

prattle *(PRAT-l), verb*
To babble; to talk nonstop without regard as to whether what you are saying makes sense or is of any interest to the listener.

"Infancy conforms to nobody: all conform to it, so that one babe commonly makes four or five out of the adults who PRATTLE and play to it." – Ralph Waldo Emerson, American poet, essayist, and transcendentalist

precarious *(prih-KAYR-ee-us), adjective*
Tenuous; positioned so as to be in danger of falling; unsecured.

"Existence is no more than the **PRECARIOUS** attainment of relevance in an intensely mobile flux of past, present, and future." – *Susan Sontag, American literary theorist, philosopher, and political activist*

precipitous *(pri-SIP-ih-tuss), adjective*
A steep drop, precarious position, unstable situation, volatile market, or rapid and sudden change.
Investors were stung Friday by a PRECIPITOUS drop in the Dow.

P

predestination *(pree-dess-tih-NAY-shun), noun*
The belief that we do not have free will, and that our lives and destinies are preordained and beyond our control.
The problem with PREDESTINATION is that whatever happens, you can say that it was meant to be, and no one can prove you wrong.

premonitory *(PREH-mahn-ih-tor-ee), adjective*
Strongly indicative of or intuiting that something is going to happen.
The Harrisons sold their stock in that company because they had a PRE-MONITORY vision that the company would soon go bankrupt.

prestidigitation *(PRESS-tih-dih-ji-TAY-shun), noun*
The performance of sleight-of-hand magic tricks.
The New Year's Eve gala at the Worthingtons included sumptuous meals, a full orchestra, and even a practitioner of PRESTIDIGITATION who amazed the children with her performance.

preternatural *(pree-tur-NACH-err-uhl), adjective*
Both supernatural and *preternatural* describe things that are out of the norm. But supernatural implies forces beyond understanding, while *preternatural* simply means abnormal or unnatural.
"I rested my knee against the cabinet for leverage and pulled hard, calling on PRETERNATURAL strength." – Mario Acevedo, American fantasy author

prima facie *(pree-ma-FAY-shuh), adjective, adverb*
Something accepted upon the face of the evidence until further examination proves or disproves it.
We have PRIMA FACIE evidence that it was Evelyn who fed those lies to the society page gossip columnists.

primordial *(pry-MORE-dee-ul), adjective*
Relating to the beginning of time or the early periods of Earth's developments.
The Summerfelds' fortune has been in the family for so long that many of us joke that it has PRIMORDIAL origins.

proctor *(PROHK-ter), noun*
One who manages or supervises another person's activities and affairs.
> *A life of luxury would be so exhausting if it weren't for the many PROC-TORS who take care of our mundane activities.*

procure *(pro-KYORE), verb*
To seek and eventually gain ownership of something.
> *My book dealer recently PROCURED, at considerable expense, a first edition of* Great Expectations *for our library.*

profligate *(PROF-lih-gayt), adjective*
Extravagant; wasteful; activity, expenditures, or indulgences beyond that which any reasonable person would desire.
> *"The official account of the Church's development viewed alternative voices as expressing the views of a misguided minority, craven followers of contemporary culture, PROFLIGATE sinners, or worse." – Harold Attridge, Dean of Yale University Divinity School*

pro forma *(pro-FOR-mah), adverb, adjective, noun*
Standard; following a commonly accepted format or process.
> *"Don't worry about reading the fine print," the manager told the young singer as he shoved the contract in front of him and put a pen in his hand. "It's just PRO FORMA."*

proletariat *(pro-leh-TARE-ee-uht), noun*
A class of society whose members earn their living solely by the exchange of their labor for money.
> *Your average dentist thinks he is upper class, but in reality, he is just another member of the PROLETARIAT.*

prolixity *(pro-LICK-sih-tee), noun*
Refers to a speech or piece of writing that is deliberately wordy and long-winded due to an ornate or formal style.
> *"The writer who loses his self-doubt, who gives way as he grows old to a sudden euphoria, to PROLIXITY, should stop writing immediately: the time has come for him to lay aside his pen." – Colette, French novelist*

promulgate *(PRAH-mull-gate), verb*
To elevate a behavior or action—or the prohibition of a particular behavior or action—to the status of a law, rule, or regulation through public decree.

The Department of Public Works PROMULGATED mandatory recycling of all paper waste in Bergen County.

propagate *(PRAH-pah-gayt), verb*
To grow, breed, or cause to multiply and flourish.

"The fiction of happiness is **PROPAGATED** by every tongue." – *Samuel Johnson, British moralist and poet*

propensity *(pro-PEN-sih-tee), noun*
A tendency to behave in a certain way.
Despite her vehement denials, Virginia has shown us a PROPENSITY toward pomposity.

propriety *(pro-PRY-ah-tee), noun*
Behaving in a way that conforms to the manners and morals of polite society.

"**PROPRIETY** is the least of all laws, and the most observed." – *François de La Rochefoucauld, French author*

propitiate *(pro-PISH-ee-ate), verb*
To win over; to gain the approval and admiration of.
"The life that went on in [many of the street's houses] seemed to me made up of evasions and negations; shifts to save cooking, to save washing and cleaning, devices to PROPITIATE the tongue of gossip." – Willa Cather, American author

proscribe *(pro-SCRIBE), transitive verb*
To forbid or prohibit; frequently confused with the word "prescribe."
State law PROSCRIBES the keeping of wild animals as house pets.

proxy *(PRAHK-see), noun*
The authority, typically in writing, to represent someone else or manage their affairs; a person authorized to act on the behalf of others.
While his mother was ill, Larry acted as her PROXY and made hospitalization decisions on her behalf.

puerile *(PYOO-er-ill), adjective*
Immature, babyish, infantile.

> *"An admiral whose PUERILE vanity has betrayed him into a testimonial . . . [is] sufficient to lure the hopeful patient to his purchase." – Samuel Hopkins Adams, American journalist*

pugnacious *(pug-NAY-shus), adjective*
Some who always wants to argue and debate every last thing.

> *Teenagers are PUGNACIOUS by nature: if I say "no," he invariably asks "why."*

purport *(per-PORT), verb*
Claiming to be something you are not; pretending to do something you aren't in fact doing.

> *"Doris Lessing PURPORTS to remember in the most minute detail the moth-eaten party dresses she pulled, at age thirteen, from her mother's trunk." – Tim Parks, British novelist*

pusillanimous *(pyoo-suh-LAN-ih-muss), adjective*
Being mild or timid by nature; a shrinking violet; a person who seeks to avoid conflict, challenge, and danger.

> *Frank L. Baum's most PUSILLANIMOUS fictional creation is the Cowardly Lion of Oz.*

pyre *(PIE-err), noun*
A pile of wood and twigs, lit on fire to burn bodies during funerals.

> *Suzette was so devastated when her fiancé ran off with another socialite that she took his belongings and burned them on a metaphorical funeral PYRE.*

pyrrhic *(PIR-ick), adjective*
A prize or victory won at the cost of an effort that exceeds its value.

> *Spending $20 at the carnival game to win his child a stuffed animal worth $5 was a PYRRHIC victory at best.*

"O the orator's joys! / To inflate the chest, to roll the thunder of the voice out from the ribs and throat, / To make the people rage, weep, hate, desire, with yourself, / To lead America—to QUELL America with a great tongue."

————

Walt Whitman, American poet
and humanist

quaff *(KWAF), verb*
To drink with gusto and in large volume.

> "We **QUAFF** the cup of life with eager haste without draining it, instead of which it only overflows the brim." *– William Hazlitt, English literary critic and philosopher*

quagmire *(KWAG-myer), noun*
A thorny problem for which there is no ready solution; a messy situation from which there is no expeditious means of escape.
> *"Your home is regarded as a model home, your life as a model life. But all this splendor, and you along with it . . . it's just as though it were built upon a shifting QUAGMIRE." – Henrik Ibsen, Norwegian playwright*

qualm *(KWAHM), noun*
A sudden feeling of uneasiness, often linked to a pang in one's conscience.
> *Of course we feel no QUALMS about wanting the finest things in life; that is the legacy our forefathers bequeathed to us.*

quandary *(KWON-duh-ree), noun*
A state of uncertainty about one's next move.
> *Estelle realized that her unrestrained comments to the society pages had left the rest of us quite upset, and she was in a QUANDARY as to how to repair the situation.*

quash *(KWAHSH), verb*
To repress or subdue completely.
> *She quickly QUASHED the rebellion of the other members of the PTO by reminding them of the superiority of her social contacts.*

quaver *(KWAY-ver), verb*
To tremble and shake from fear, excitement, etc.
> *Eloise positively QUAVERED as she made her debut at her coming out party.*

quean *(KWEEN), noun*
A disreputable woman; a prostitute.
> *Esmerelda can act like such a QUEAN when her boyfriends do not automatically give her the luxury items she requires.*

quell (KWELL), verb

To suppress or extinguish; or, to quiet one's own or another's anxieties.

"O the orator's joys! / To inflate the chest, to roll the thunder of the voice out from the ribs and throat, / To make the people rage, weep, hate, desire, with yourself, / To lead America—to QUELL America with a great tongue." – Walt Whitman, American poet and humanist

querulous (KWER-eh-luss), adjective

Describes a person who continually whines and complains about practically everything.

Their QUERULOUS manner with the waiter made them unpleasant and embarrassing dinner companions.

quibble (KWIB-ul), noun

To argue over a minor matter; to voice a niggling objection.

If you are not 100 percent satisfied, your money will promptly be refunded without question or QUIBBLE.

quid pro quo (KWID-pro-kwo), noun

A fair exchange of assets or services; a favor given in return for something of equal value.

In a QUID PRO QUO, Stephen helped Alex with his math homework, while Alex did Stephen's chores.

quiescent (kwee-ESS-ehnt), adjective

Being at rest, inactive, or motionless.

"There is a brief time for sex, and a long time when sex is out of place. But when it is out of place as an activity there still should be the large and quiet space in the consciousness where it lives QUIESCENT." – D. H. Lawrence, British author

quietus (kwy-EET-uhs), noun

Something that ends or settles a situation.

"For who would bare the whips and scorns of time, / Th'oppressor's wrong, the proud man's contumely, / The pangs of disprized love, the law's delay, / The insolence of office, and the spurns / That patient merit of th'unworthy takes, / When he himself might his **QUIETUS** make / With a bare bodkin?" – *William Shakespeare*

quintessential *(KWIN-tuh-sen-shul), adjective*
The most perfect or typical example of its category or kind.
> *"Craving that old sweet oneness yet dreading engulfment, wishing to be our mother's and yet be our own, we stormily swing from mood to mood, advancing and retreating—the QUINTESSENTIAL model of two-mindedness." – Judith Viorst, American author and psychoanalyst*

quirk *(KWIHRK), noun*
A peculiarity of one's personality or manner.
> *One of the most omnipresent QUIRKS of the nouveau riche is that they still ask the price of a luxury item, rather than simply offering to purchase it.*

quisling *(KWIZ-ling), noun*
A traitor; a person who conspires with the enemy.
> *The leader of Norway's National Unity movement was executed for being a QUISLING in 1945.*

quixotic *(kwik-SOT-ick), adjective*
A person or team pursuing a seemingly unreachable or at least extremely ambitious and difficult goal—one considered by many to be either idealist, impractical, or both.
> *"There is something QUIXOTIC in me about money, something meek and guilty. I want it and like it. But I cannot imagine insisting on it, pressing it out of people." – Brenda Ueland, American author*

quizzical *(KWIHZ-ih-kuhl), adjective*
Unusual or comical; or, puzzled.
> *The QUIZZICAL look on Amanda's face, when David trailed a marriage-proposal banner behind his private plane, was absolutely priceless.*

quondam *(KWAHN-dumm), adjective*
Former; at-one-time.
> *You should not hire the Wilkersons' QUONDAM servant because she has been known to break many objets d'art.*

quotidian *(kwo-TID-ee-an), adjective*
Familiar; commonplace; nothing out of the ordinary.
> *Despite closets full of the latest Parisian couture, Alison's QUOTIDIAN complaint is that she has "nothing to wear."*

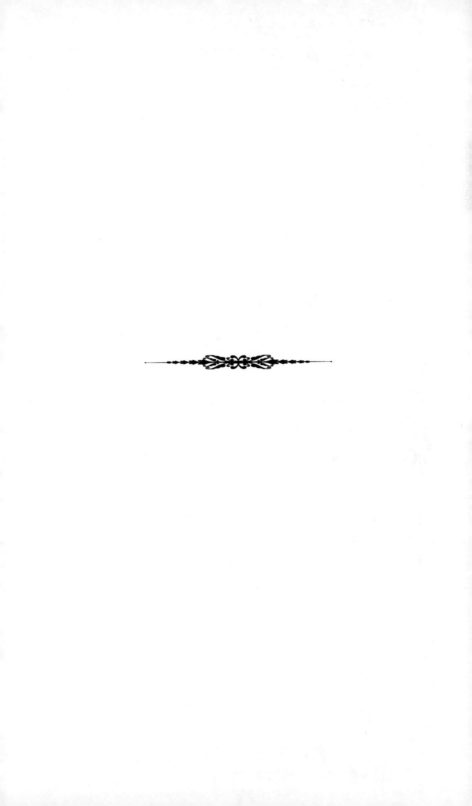

"The mind that's conscious of its RECTITUDE, / Laughs at the lies of rumor."

——•——

Ovid, Roman poet

R

raconteur *(RAH-kon-tour), noun*
Someone who enjoys telling stories, does so frequently, and is good at it.
> *"O'Hara writes as a poetic one-man band, shifting rapidly among his roles as RACONTEUR, sexual adventurer, European traveler . . ."* – Edward Mendelson, Professor of English and Comparative Literature at Colombia University

raillery *(RAIL-err-ee), noun*
Good-natured teasing.
> *"RAILLERY," said Montesquieu, "is a way of speaking in favor of one's wit at the expense of one's better nature."*

raiment *(RAY-muhnt), noun*
Clothing or apparel of the finest quality.
> *When Priscilla entered the room attired in RAIMENT of pure gold, her guests gasped and more than one glass of wine was overturned on silken tablecloths.*

raison d'être *(RAY-zohn-deh-truh), noun*
The core reason why something exists; its central purpose and mission in this world.
> *When Jane's children went off to college, her RAISON D'ÊTRE disappeared, and she fell into a deep depression.*

rambunctious *(ram-BUHNGK-shuhss), adjective*
Difficult to handle; wild and boisterous.
> *"The golden age, when RAMBUNCTIOUS spirits were regarded as the source of evil."* – Friedrich Nietzsche, nineteenth-century German philosopher

ramification *(ram-uh-fuh-KAY-shun), noun*
A natural consequence of an action or circumstance.
> *A RAMIFICATION of a prolonged stay in low or zero gravity would be loss of bone mass and lean muscle.*

rancor *(RAYN-core), noun*
Conflict between individuals or groups, usually resulting from disagreement over an action or issue, and accompanied by ill will, bad feelings, and an escalation of the dispute over time.
> *"They no longer assume responsibility (as beat cops used to do) for averting RANCOR between antagonistic neighbors."* – Harlan Ellison, American author

rapacity *(ruh-PAH-sih-tee), noun*
Greed for wealth, power, fame, and success, even at the expense of others.
> *An unquenchable desire for the finer things in life is not RAPACITY, as some have suggested. It is, instead, a mark of higher birth.*

rapprochement *(rah-PROWCH-ment), noun*
Re-establishment of friendly relations between nations following a period of hostility.
> *Lydia spoke at length about how RAPPROCHEMENT between the United States and some former Soviet nations has been a real boon to her family's prestige and wealth.*

rarefied *(RARE-uh-fyed), adjective*
Lofty; exalted; of high class or caliber.
> *Most copywriters don't operate in the RAREFIED environment in which Clayton makes his millions.*

ratiocinate *(ray-shee-OSS-inn-ate), verb*
To work toward the solution of a problem through logical thinking and reason.
> *Since the dawn of humanity, our best minds have failed to RATIOCI-NATE a method of proving God's existence.*

raze *(RAYZ), verb*
To tear down or demolish.
> *We had to RAZE our Cape Cod home and rebuild it entirely, due to some structural damage to the home caused by high winds.*

recalcitrant *(rih-KAL-sih-trunt), adjective*
Unwilling to cooperate voluntarily; hesitant to step forward and do what one is asked or told to do.
> *On the witness stand, the mobster was RECALCITRANT and uncommunicative.*

recant *(rih-KANT), verb*
To withdraw or disavow formally.
> *"I cannot and will not RECANT anything, for to go against conscience is neither right nor safe." – Martin Luther, the father of Protestantism*

recapitulate *(ree-kah-PIT-chew-late), verb*
To repeat something, but in a more concise form.

"To RECAPITULATE: always be on time for my class," the professor told his freshman class on the first day of the semester.

recession *(ree-SESH-in), noun*
A troubled economy characterized by a decline in gross domestic product for two consecutive quarters; a period during which unemployment is on the rise, inflation is increasing, and consumer confidence and spending power is eroded.

The looming RECESSION has even hurt some of our families, who have had to let go of second yachts and one or two homes.

reciprocity *(res-uh-PROS-ih-tee), noun*
Doing business with—or a favor for—someone, because they have done a favor for, or bought from, you.

Giving customers free gifts increases sales because of the principle of RECIPROCITY.

recompense *(REE-kum-pense), verb, noun*
To give someone cash or something else of value to make up for injury or inconvenience they suffered at your hands, either accidentally or deliberately.

"To be remembered after we are dead, is but poor **RECOMPENSE** for being treated with contempt while we are living." – *William Hazlitt, English literary critic and philosopher*

recondite *(REHK-un-dite), adjective*
Beyond typical knowledge and understanding.

For most people, opera, polo, and fine wine remain RECONDITE subjects.

recriminate *(rih-KRIM-uh-nayt), verb*
To bring up accusations against someone who has accused you.

After Natasha was snubbed by us for blabbing to the gossip pages, she RECRIMINATED by pointing out that some of us had leaked gossip ourselves.

rectitude *(REHK-ti-tood), noun*
Moral virtue; rightness.

"The mind that's conscious of its RECTITUDE, / Laughs at the lies of rumor." – Ovid, Roman poet

recumbent *(rih-KUHM-bent), adjective*
Inactive, idle; lying down.
> *During our Italian cruise, we spent most of our time RECUMBENT on the bow of the yacht, soaking up the sun's rays.*

recursive *(ree-KURSS-iv), adjective*
Pertaining to a process in which each step makes use of the results of the earlier steps.
> *The study of mathematics is a RECURSIVE learning experience.*

R

redact *(re-DAKT), verb*
To edit a comment, thought, or written document before going public with it.
> *"You may want to REDACT your opinion on your opponent's health care policies," his campaign manager warned him.*

redolent *(RED-oh-lent), adjective*
An object possessing a rich scent or alluring aroma, or a situation with a hint or promise of rich possibilities.
> *Her rose garden was REDOLENT with the perfume of a thousand flowers.*

redoubtable *(rih-DOW-tuh-bull), adjective*
The quality of being a formidable opponent.
> *Michael's REDOUBTABLE nature made him a successful negotiator and trial attorney.*

reflexive *(reh-FLEK-siv), adjective*
Something that happens through reflex rather than deliberate choice or effort.
> *We don't mean to act imperiously toward the nouveau riche; it's just a REFLEXIVE and conditioned response.*

refulgent *(rih-FUHL-jent), adjective*
Radiant, gleaming; shining brightly.
> *When Anastasia moved her bejeweled hand while lounging in the mid-day sunshine, her sparkling diamonds were REFULGENT.*

rejoinder *(rih-JOIN-der), noun*
A clever or witty reply to a question or comment.
> *Lydia's often catty REJOINDERS quickly made her the bane of our group.*

remiss *(rih-miss), adjective*
Negligent or careless.
> *Our servants know that if they ever are REMISS in their duties, then we will quickly fire them.*

R

remittance *(ree-MITT-inss), noun*
A payment for goods or services purchased on credit.
> *Lacking a credit card, he made a REMITTANCE on his account online using PayPal.*

remonstrate *(rih-MON-strate), verb*
To protest, object, or to show disapproval.
> *When Carlotta REMONSTRATED our snubbing of Julia, we simply began to snub Carlotta as well.*

remunerate *(rih-MYOO-nuh-rate), verb*
To settle a debt or other financial obligation by making a payment.
> *Peter's supervisor at the insurance company would do anything to avoid REMUNERATING policyholders for the claims they made.*

renaissance *(REN-ah-sonce), noun, adjective*
A period of great learning, thinking, and creativity—in art, literature, science, economics, and philosophy.
> *We were so pleased by the RENAISSANCE of wealth acquisition that arose during the closing years of the twentieth century.*

renunciation *(ree-nun-see-AYE-shun), noun*
To distance yourself from a position or belief; to publicly state a shift in ideals or position on an issue while criticizing your past stance as wrong.
> *"With RENUNCIATION life begins." – Amelia E. Barr, British novelist*

reparations *(reh-par-AYE-shins), noun*
Payments made by nations defeated in war to the victors, who impose these payments to recover from some of the costs of battle.
> *After World War I, REPARATIONS of 132 billion gold marks were imposed on Germany by the French.*

repartee *(rep-er-TAY), noun*
Conversation characterized by witty banter.
> *Our galas and balls are always marked by delightful REPARTEE around the grand dinner table.*

repertoire *(REH-per-tware), noun*
A library of works that a group knows and regularly performs.
> *The philharmonic's REPERTOIRE includes most of the classical standards from Bach, Beethoven, Brahms, and Mozart.*

replete *(rih-PLEET), adjective*
Abundantly provided; complete.

> "The highway is **REPLETE** with culinary land mines disguised as quaint local restaurants that carry such reassuring names as Millie's, Pop's and Capt'n Dick's." – *Bryan Miller, American food critic*

repose *(rih-POHZ), noun*
To be in a position or state of rest.

> The wholesome relief, **REPOSE**, content; / And this bunch, pluck'd at random from myself; / It has done its work—I tossed it carelessly to fall where it may. – *Walt Whitman, American poet and humanist*

reprobate *(REE-pro-bait), noun*
A person who routinely commits illegal, immoral, or unethical acts without hesitation or remorse.
> *One reason that Anthony continues to be a REPROBATE is because his father, as well as his social contacts, keep bailing him out of jail.*

reprove *(ree-PROOV), verb*
To criticize and correct others.
> *We found it necessary to REPROVE Elyssia for some of her questionable fashion choices.*

repudiate *(reh-pew-dee-AYTE),verb*
To dispute an idea, decision, or belief; to distance oneself and refuse to be associated with someone or something.
> *We repeatedly REPUDIATED James for his assertion that Rolex watches surpass those of Cartier.*

requisite *(REK-wiz-it), noun or adjective*
A mandatory action, requirement, or condition; or, necessary and mandatory.
Being physically fit is a REQUISITE to getting a job as a firefighter.

requite *(rih-KWYTE), verb*
To seek revenge for an actual or assumed wrong.
". . . certain sets of human beings are very apt to maintain that other sets should give up their lives to them and their service, and then they REQUITE them by praise" – Charlotte Brönte, British novelist

rescind *(ree-SINNED), verb*
Take away, revoke, cancel, withdraw, remove.
Richard RESCINDED his order for a yacht, opting instead to purchase a private aircraft.

respite *(RESS-pit), noun*
A temporary delay from something distressing.

"Sweet Flower of Hope! free Nature's genial child! / That didst so fair disclose thy early bloom, / Filling the wide air with a rich perfume! / For thee in vain all heavenly aspects smiled; / From the hard world brief **RESPITE** could they win . . ." – *Samuel Taylor Coleridge, English poet*

resplendent *(reh-SPLEN-dent), adjective*
Garbed or decorated in lush fabrics and rich, vibrant colors.
The bride was RESPLENDENT in a beaded silk gown.

restive *(RESS-tihv), adjective*
Impatient and stubborn.
Audrey was so worked up about her first summer abroad that her excitement came across as RESTIVE.

reticent *(REH-tih-scent), adjective*
Reluctance to openly express one's thoughts, feelings, and personal business to other people; behaving like an introvert in social situations.
"The shorter poems tend to be RETICENT, psychologically acute love poems about the shifting inequalities of love." – Edward Mendelson, Professor of English and Comparative Literature at Colombia University

retinue *(RET-n-oo)*, *noun*
A group of people who follow an important person either because they desire to do so or because it is their job to do so.
> *A Secret Service RETINUE follows the President wherever he goes, twenty-four hours a day.*

retort *(rih-TORT)*, *verb*, *noun*
To reply in a sharp, retaliatory manner.
> *Carl had to bite back a sharp RETORT when Sallee criticized the couture gown his mother wore to the soiree.*

retrograde *(REH-trow-grayed)*, *adjective*
Reverting to an earlier state, condition, or style; harkening to an earlier time and place.
> *My favorite diner is decorated in a RETROGRADE art deco style.*

revelry *(REV-uhl-ree)*, *noun*
Boisterous festivity and merrymaking.

> "Midnight shout and **REVELRY**, / Tipsy dance and jollity." – *John Milton, English poet*

rhetoric *(REH-tore-ik)*, *noun*
Artful use of language to get other people to see your point of view; making a persuasive case more through persuasive speech or writing than with actual facts and evidence.
> *Plato called RHETORIC "the art of ruling the minds of men."*

ribald *(RIB-uld)*, *adjective*
Lewd; off-color; somewhat dirty and inappropriate.
> *"It is . . . useful to distinguish between the pornographic, condemned in every society, and the bawdy, the RIBALD, the shared vulgarities and jokes, which are the safety valves of most social systems." – Margaret Mead, American cultural anthropologist*

rife *(RIFE)*, *adjective*
Prevalent, abundant, abounding.
> *The hotel was RIFE with tourists, so we quickly went upstairs to the penthouse.*

rigmarole *(RIG-muh-roll), noun*
Absurdly complicated procedures and instructions; a bunch of unnecessary baloney.
> *The club had some value to him in business, but he quickly grew tired of all the RIGMAROLE at meetings.*

riposte *(rih-POST), noun*
A quick, often witty or cutting, response to a comment or question.
> *Eileen was unable to offer one of her usual RIPOSTES when we descried her decision to eschew the season's fashion.*

risible *(RIZZ-uh-bull), adjective*
Capable of causing laughter due to its ludicrous nature.
> *Janine's decision to summer in the Hamptons instead of on the French Riviera was deemed RISIBLE by the rest of us.*

roisterers *(ROY-stir-ers), noun*
Partiers, celebrators, or an individual or group having a good time in a loud and boisterous manner.
> *The ROISTERERS' enjoyment of the party was so infectious, their neighbors joined them instead of complaining about the noise.*

roué *(roo-AY), noun*
A dissolute man in fashionable society; a rake.
> *"A pretty wife is something for the fastidious vanity of a ROUÉ to retire upon." – Thomas Moore, Irish poet and songwriter*

rubric *(ROO-brick), noun*
A class, category, title, or heading.
> *We decided to place Natasha's ball gown under the RUBRIC of "failed fashion choices."*

rue *(ROO), verb*
To repent of and regret bitterly.
> *Elliott knew he would RUE the day that he decided to sell his Maserati, but he did so at his father's urging.*

rumination *(ROO-muh-nay-shun), noun*
The act of thinking about something in great detail, weighing the pros and cons over and over in your mind.

> *For busy people under stress, RUMINATION after going to bed is a frequent contributor to insomnia.*

ruritanian *(roor-ih-TAYNE-ee-in), adjective*
Anything related to a romantic adventure or its environment.

> *The two lovers found Barbados to be a RURITANIAN paradise.*

"It is natural to indulge in the illusions of hope. We are apt to shut our eyes to that SIREN until she 'allures' us to our death."

———

Gertrude Stein, American author

sacrilegious *(sack-reh-LIIH-juss), adjective*
Openly insulting or disrespectful to the beliefs, religion, ideas, and practices of others—especially the ones they hold most sacred.

Bryson's insistence that Miró is more collectible that Warhol is positively SACRILEGIOUS.

sacrosanct *(SACK-roh-sankt), adjective*
Beyond criticism because it is considered sacred.

"If men could get pregnant, maternity benefits would be as SACRO-SANCT as the G.I. Bill." – Letty Cottin Pogrebin. American editor and writer

sagacity *(suh-GASS-ih-tee), noun*
Wisdom; soundness of judgment.

"Our minds are endowed by nature with such activity and SAGAC-ITY that the soul is believed to be produced from heaven." – Quintilian, Roman rhetorician

salacious *(suh-LAY-shuss), adjective*
Having an unhealthy, obsessive, or addictive interest in sex.

For weeks, the society pages were rife with SALACIOUS gossip, which turned out to originate from Mallory, who had lost her beau to Jeannette.

salient *(SALE-yent), adjective*
Relevant; germane; important; something that stands out and gets noticed.

The pond in the front yard is the most SALIENT feature of our new home.

salubrious *(suh-LOO-bree-us), adjective*
Favorable to one's health.

After father's asthma reasserted itself, the family began to spend more time at its Arizona compound due to the area's dry weather, which is SALUBRIOUS toward asthmatics.

salutary *(SAL-you-tar-ee), adjective*
To have a soothing or healing effect; an act that helps one recover or benefit from a situation.

Tuberculosis patients were often sent to the mountains, where the fresh air was thought to have a SALUTARY effect on their condition.

sanctimonious *(sank-tih-MOAN-ee-us), adjective*
Overbearingly self-righteous and smug in the (perhaps mistaken) belief that one's opinion is correct, and possessing an air of moral superiority about one's opinion.

> "Not but I've every reason not to care / What happens to him if it only takes / Some of the **SANCTIMONIOUS** conceit / Out of one of those pious scalawags." – *Robert Frost, American poet*

sangfroid *(san-FWAH), noun*
The attitude or state of possessing a cool head and steadfast composure in the face of danger, adversity, or stressful situations.
The car crash shook him, but within seconds he recovered his SANG-FROID and went to check on his driver.

sanguine *(SANG-gwihn), adjective*
Accepting of circumstances with good cheer and a positive attitude.
"Many marketers were SANGUINE about the Do Not Call introduction, saying that it helped better focus their telephone communications."
– Eleanor Trickett, DM News *editor*

sapient *(SAY-pee-ent), adjective*
Wise.
The judge made a SAPIENT ruling in splitting custody between the two parents.

sardonic *(sar-DON-ik), adjective*
Mean-spirited sarcasm.
When I asked the bank for another home equity loan, the president, who was called out of his office by the teller, approached with a SARDONIC grin.

sartorial *(sar-TOR-ee-al), adjective*
Anything related to the way a person dresses, typically used to describe a man who wears finely tailored clothing.
Jonathan's personal tailor always makes sure that Jonathan radiates SARTORIAL splendor.

satiety *(suh-TIE-ih-tee), noun*
The sensation or feeling of being full or having eaten too much.
Although we knew we would be struck by SATIETY, we could not resist the gustatory delights offered at the Whittington's New Year's gala.

saturnine *(SAT-ur-neen), adjective*
Moody; morose; gloomy; unhappy; having a pessimistic outlook on life.
> *Ever since his father told him he could not have another Lotus Esprit, Williams has acted positively SATURNINE.*

satyr *(SAY-ter), noun*
A lascivious, lecherous man.
> *Harold's graceful manners disappear once he has had a few glasses of champagne, and he becomes a veritable SATYR.*

savant *(sah-VANT), noun*
A person with a natural talent or genius in a particular field or skill.
> *With her family's background in finance, it was a given that Francine would be a Wall Street SAVANT.*

savoir faire *(SAV-wahr-FAIR), noun*
An evident sense of confidence, optimism, and proficiency in the task at hand.
> *Eileen hosted a charity luncheon for forty people with her usual SAVOIR FAIRE.*

scarify *(SKARE-ih-fie), verb*
To wound with harsh criticism.
> *We deemed it necessary to SCARIFY Eileen for having the nerve to criticize our fashion sense.*

scintilla *(SIN-tih-lah), noun*
A spark; a tiny trace amount.
> *"The air twittered with bright SCINTILLAS of fading light."* – Harlan Ellison, American author

scion *(SIGH-uhn), noun*
A descendant or heir.

> **"SCION** of chiefs and monarchs, where art thou? / Fond hope of many nations, art thou dead?" – *Lord Byron, British Romantic poet*

sectarian *(sek-TAYR-ee-in), adjective*
Relating to the practices, nature, or activities of a sect.
> *"In the early 1990s, as the insurgency took on a more unambiguously religious and SECTARIAN flavor, several Pandits were killed, and most of the rest fled for their lives."* – William Dalrymple, Scottish historian and author

secular *(SEK-yuh-lehr), adjective*
Separate from or devoid of religious belief or connotation.
> *"The liberal humanist assumption that American society, like that of Europe, would become progressively SECULAR was always something of a delusion." – Gordon Wood, History Professor at Brown University*

sedentary *(SEHD-n-tare-ee), adjective*
Resting a great deal and taking little exercise.
> *All we have to do is hire a personal trainer if our SEDENTARY habits begin to have negative effects on our well-being.*

sedition *(sih-DISH-uhn), noun*
An action that promotes discontent or rebellion.
> *In an act of childish SEDITION, Alex quit the club after we refused to play a round of golf with him.*

sentient *(SEN-tea-ent), adjective*
Possessing enough intelligence to be self aware.
> *"Many years ago, a particular creature was selected to develop into the dominant life form on this planet. It was given certain breaks and certain challenges, all of which, when utilized or overcome, marked it indelibly with particular traits as it moved along the road to a higher SENTIENCE." – Roger Zelazny, American science fiction writer*

separatists *(SEP-prah-tists), noun*
Those who believe a particular region or group should be separated from a larger whole.
> *Some SEPARATIST Canadians want Quebec to be a separate nation from the rest of Canada.*

sepulchral *(suh-PUHL-kruhl), adjective*
Hollow and deep; characteristic of a tomb; often used to describe certain voices.
> *Our butler's SEPULCHRAL voice instantly impresses our social contacts when they come to visit.*

sequester *(see-KWESS-ter), verb*
To remove and isolate a portion from a larger whole.
> *"A great deal of genetic engineering must be done before we have carbon-eaters SEQUESTING carbon in sufficient quantity to counteract the burning of fossil fuels." – Freeman Dyson, English-born American physicist and mathematician*

serendipity *(ser-en-DIP-it-ee), noun*
Attaining success, good fortune, or the object of your desire more through luck and random circumstance than deliberate effort.

>*What made him an Internet billionaire was SERENDIPITY more than brains or talent.*

serpentine *(SUR-pen-teen), adjective*
Snake-like in shape or movement.

>"For it is not possible to join **SERPENTINE** wisdom with columbine innocency, except men know exactly all the conditions of the serpent."
>*– Francis Bacon, English philosopher, author, and statesman*

sesquipedalian *(ses-kwi-pih-DAL-yin), adjective*
A writer or speaker who prefers big, complex words and arcane jargon to plain, simple English, or a piece of writing containing such prose.

>*"Recently a strange whimsy has started to creep in among the SESQUI-PEDALIAN prose of scientific journals." – Stephen Hall, American architect*

sidereal *(SIGH-der-eel), adjective*
Determined by outside forces, particularly the positions of the stars and planets in the evening sky.

>*"Thoughts give birth to a creative force that is neither elemental nor SIDEREAL." – Philippus Paracelsus, Swiss alchemist, astrologer, and physician*

sinecure *(SIN-eh-KYOOR), noun*
A job or office without regular duties but with regular pay; a position requiring minimal labor but conveying prestige or status to one who holds it.

>*Being elected as the new president of his trade association bestowed on Bill some much-needed SINECURE.*

siren *(SY-ren), noun*
A destructive, but seductively beautiful, beguiling woman; or, anything considered dangerously seductive.

>*"It is natural to indulge in the illusions of hope. We are apt to shut our eyes to that SIREN until she 'allures' us to our death." – Gertrude Stein, American author*

soi-disant *(soy-dih-SAHNT)*, *adjective*
Self-styled.
> *A SOI-DISANT lady's man, Gary's focus was always on his next conquest.*

sojourn *(SO-jern)*, *noun*
A temporary visit or stay.
> *The Israelites' SOJOURN in the desert lasted for forty long years.*

solidarity *(sol-ih-DARE-ih-tee)*, *noun*
Bonding of people to others because of shared interests, beliefs, goals, or attitudes.
> *"It was the middle-class female SOLIDARITY, defending a nice girl from charges of calculation and viciousness." – Saul Bellow, American author*

soliloquy *(suh-LIL-ih-kwee)*, *noun*
A dramatic or literary form of speaking in which a character reveals his innermost thoughts when he is alone or thinks he is alone.
> *The most famous SOLILOQUY in all of literature is the "To be or not to be" speech in Hamlet.*

solipsism *(SAHL-ip-sihz-uhm)*, *noun*
The notion that one's own experiences and thoughts are the only source of true knowledge.
> *The SOLIPSISM of some members of the leisure class is distasteful to those of us who, for example, know what our servants need even more than they do.*

solstice *(SOUL-stis)*, *noun*
A day of the year during which the sun is at its highest or lowest point in the sky, causing the shortest day of the year on December 21 (winter *solstice*) and the longest day of the year on June 21 (summer *solstice*).
> *We open our lake house for the summer season every year at the SOLSTICE.*

sonorous *(SON-er-russ)*, *adjective*
A deep, rich, resonant sound.
> *The b-flat bass saxophone is the most SONOROUS member of the saxophone family, with the baritone saxophone coming in a close second.*

sophist *(SAHF-ist), adjective*
Sounding reasonable, yet patently false.
> *One can argue that what is learned in law school is largely the skill of making SOPHIST arguments that a jury can believe.*

soporific *(sop-uh-RIFF-ick), adjective*
Something so boring, tedious, or exhausting that it makes one start to fall asleep.
> *If Cassandra weren't such an important social contact, her SOPORIFIC speech would surely cause us to avoid her.*

specious *(SPEE-shus), adjective*
Something that appears correct on the surface, but is in fact wrong.
> *The judge summarily rejected the SPECIOUS arguments put forth by the defendant, which seemed to have no evidence to back them up.*

spoonerism *(SPOON-er-iz-um), noun*
A phrase in which the syllables of neighboring words are accidentally interchanged.
> *A popular SPOONERISM states: "Cook a grilled cheese sandwich in lots of butter, let it get cold, and you have a chilled grease sandwich."*

Sphinx *(SFINKS), noun*
A mythical creature with the head of a woman, the body of a lion, the wings of an eagle, and the tail of a serpent.
> *When Oedipus correctly answered the SPHINX'S riddle, the SPHINX leaped to its death in the valley below.*

spurious *(SPYOOR-ee-us), adjective*
False; inauthentic; not well thought out.
> *Every week I get SPURIOUS accusations of being a spammer even though my list is entirely double opt-in.*

stagnation *(stag-NAY-shin), noun*
The condition of being inactive or the slowing of forward progress or lessening of activity.
> *"Economists' statistical techniques are not refined enough to analyze unambiguously the causes of this long-term STAGNATION." – Jeff Madrick, director of policy research at the Schwartz Center for Economic Policy Analysis, The New School.*

staid *(STAYD), adjective*
Fixed and settled; not distinctive; uninteresting.
Even though the Sandersons are an important family, we could hardly last the requisite hour at the family's STAID winter ball.

stalwart *(STAL-wart), noun, adjective*
A loyal, reliable member of an organization; a staunch supporter of a group or cause.
Although Wayne is no longer a working engineer, he is a STALWART member of the American Institute of Chemical Engineers.

stoicism *(STOH-ih-si-zum), noun*
Enduring pain or suffering without complaining.
"He soldiered through his duties with what looked like cheerful STO-ICISM." – Thomas Pynchon, American author

stolid *(STAHL-id), adjective*
Unemotional and impassive.
Thomas's STOLID demeanor hides the heart of a jet-setting playboy.

stringent *(STRIHN-juhnt), adjective*
Rigorous, strict, severe.

> "No laws, however **STRINGENT**, can make the idle industrious, the thriftless provident, or the drunken sober." – *Samuel Smiles, Scottish author and reformer*

strophe *(STROF), noun*
A stanza containing lines that do not conform to the type, style, or form of the poem in which they appear.
Those not wearing haute couture stick out at our gatherings like STRO-PHES stick out in short poems.

stultify *(STUHL-tuh-fie), verb*
To cause to appear foolish or ridiculous.
The out-of-date chapeau absolutely STULTIFIED Heather's otherwise immaculate couture.

stygian *(STY-gee-an), adjective*
Eerily quiet, so dark as to be almost pitch black.

"STAND close around, ye **STYGIAN** set, / With Dirce in one boat convey'd! / Or Charon, seeing, may forget / That he is old and she a shade" – *Walter Savage Landor, British writer and poet*

subjugation *(sub-jih-GAY-shun), noun*
The process of making someone your inferior and requiring them to take orders from you.
"There was a flavor of SUBJUGATION in his love for Madeleine." – Saul Bellow, American author

sublime *(suh-BLYME), adjective*
Reaching new levels of quality and perfection unduplicated elsewhere; of such immense beauty that the viewer's breath is taken away, metaphorically speaking.
"The SUBLIME and the ridiculous are often so nearly related, that it is difficult to class them separately. One step above the SUBLIME makes the ridiculous, and one step above the ridiculous makes the SUBLIME again." – Thomas Paine, English revolutionary and intellectual

subliminal *(sub-LIM-inn-uhl), adjective*
Operating below the threshold of consciousness, but still having an affect on the mind.
SUBLIMINAL advertising was a big fad in advertising in the 1970s.

subrogation *(suh-bro-GAY-shin), noun*
The substitution of one person for another with respect to a lawful claim or right.
The SUBROGATION clause in the lease says that if the landlord cannot collect rent from the tenant, she has the right to collect from the co-signer of the leasing agreement.

subsistence *(SUB-sis-tense), noun*
The minimum—of food, water, clothing, shelter, and money—a person or family needs to survive.
All we need for SUBSISTENCE is the basics: the finest of everything.

subversive *(sub-VER-siv), adjective*
Describes an act performed to challenge or overthrow the authority of those in power.

"If sex and creativity are often seen by dictators as SUBVERSIVE activities, it's because they lead to the knowledge that you own your own body."
– Erica Jong, American author and teacher

suffrage *(SUF-rij), noun*
The right to vote in political elections.

"Higginson was an early advocate of women's SUFFRAGE as he was a vociferous advocate of civil rights for Negroes." – Joyce Carol Oates, American author

sultry *(SUL-tree), adjective*
In terms of weather, hot and humid, with little or no breeze. In terms of human behavior, suggestive of passion or smoldering sexuality.

"Bare-headed in the SULTRY sun, Ahab stood on the bowsprit." – Herman Melville, American author

supercilious *(sue-per-SILL-ee-us), adjective*
Feeling superior to others, and as a result, having a low opinion of or contempt for them based on your belief that they are inferior.

Too many get-rich-quick promoters imbue their advertisements with a SUPERCILIOUS attitude toward the wealth seekers they profess to wanting to help.

superfluous *(soo-PER-flew-us), adjective*
Excessive and unnecessary.

Some people never seem to be aware that wearing more than a hint of fine jewelry is SUPERFLUOUS.

superlative *(sue-PURR-lah-tiv), adjective*
The quality of something's being the best in its class or quality.

Our family's show horses are SUPERLATIVE to the rest of the horses one can find in the county.

supersede *(sue-per-SEED), verb*
When one thing takes the place of another or renders the former obsolete.

"The classical laws [of physics] were SUPERSEDED by quantum laws."
– Stephen Hawking, British theoretical physicist

supplant *(suh-PLANT), verb*
To take the place of.
> *"If we would SUPPLANT the opinions and policy of our fathers in any case, we should do so upon evidence so conclusive, and arguments so clear, that even their great authority fairly considered and weighted, cannot stand."* – Abraham Lincoln

surfeit *(SUR-fit), noun*
Having too much of a good thing, especially generous servings of food and drink.
> *"A SURFEIT of the sweetest things / The deepest loathing to the stomach brings."* – William Shakespeare

surreal *(suh-REEL), adjective*
Possessing a quality that makes something seem unreal; strange; bizarre; almost other-worldly.

> "He seemed to toss them all into the mixed salads of his poetry with the same indifference to form and logic, the same domesticated **SURREALISM**, that characterized much of the American avant-garde of the period." – *Frank O'Hara, American poet*

surreptitious *(suh-rep-TISH-us), adjective*
Done in secret.
> *With little more than SURREPTITIOUS glances, Alison was able to entice Quentin to her side at the spring gala.*

susurration *(soo-suh-RAY-shun), noun*
A soft sound such as the murmuring from a hushed conversation in the next room or the rain gently falling on the roof.
> *He bought a device to help him sleep: an electronic synthesizer that mimics the SUSURRATION of a drizzle or a rainstorm.*

suzerainty *(suh-ZER-ant-tee), noun*
Paramount, unquestioned authority.
> *"The account executives are sufficiently mature to manage every phase of their accounts without challenging the ultimate SUZERAINTY of the copywriter."* – David Ogilvy, British advertising executive

sybaritic *(sih-bar-IT-ik), adjective*
Relating to self-indulgent sensuous luxury and pleasure.
Selena rubbed the suntan lotion over her tanned middle slowly, and the whole thing had an erotic, SYBARITIC quality that made the men's eyes pop out of their heads.

sycophant *(SIK-uh-fuhnt), noun*
A person attempting to get on your good side by constantly sucking up and flattering you.
Outwardly polite, the rock star secretly viewed his fans as slobbering SYCOPHANTS.

symbiosis *(sim-bee-OH-sis), noun*
A close interdependency between two organisms from two different species.
The nouveau riche would like to believe they have a SYMBIOSIS with us, but, in fact, they remain wholly separate and distinct.

synchronous *(SIN-kro-nus), adjective*
Two events or processes that take place at the same time.
The Smythingtons and the Lyttons caused quite a stir among their social contacts after they scheduled SYNCHRONOUS galas.

syncopation *(sin-ko-PAY-shun), noun*
Music in which the beats are reversed: the normally loud beats are softer, and the beats normally subdued are emphasized.
The weird SYNCOPATION in the score made the music very difficult for the percussionists to follow.

syncretistic *(sin-kre-TIH-stik), adjective*
A set of beliefs obtained by combining elements of multiple cultures, religions, societies, or schools of thought.
Pauline's SYNCRETISTIC worldview comes from the fact that her family has traveled extensively across the globe.

synecdoche *(sih-NECK-duh-kee), noun*
A type of shorthand speech in which a partial description is understood by the reader or listener to represent the whole; e.g., saying "New York" in a discussion of baseball when you mean "the New York Yankees."
Marla could not stop using a SYNECDOCHE after she returned from her trip to England at which she met the royal family, saying repeatedly that she had met and socialized with "the crown."

synoptic *(sin-OP-tik), adjective*
Forming or involving a synopsis or summary.
> *The close of a presentation should be SYNOPTIC in nature.*

systemic *(sih-STEM-ik), adjective*
Relating to a system as a whole and not just its component parts.
> *The discarding of couture clothing that is less than a year old has become SYSTEMIC among our group.*

syzygy *(SIZE-ih-gee), noun*
In astronomy, *syzygy* takes place when the Earth, sun, and moon all line up along a straight path.
> *Astronomers predict an eclipse for the next SYZYGY.*

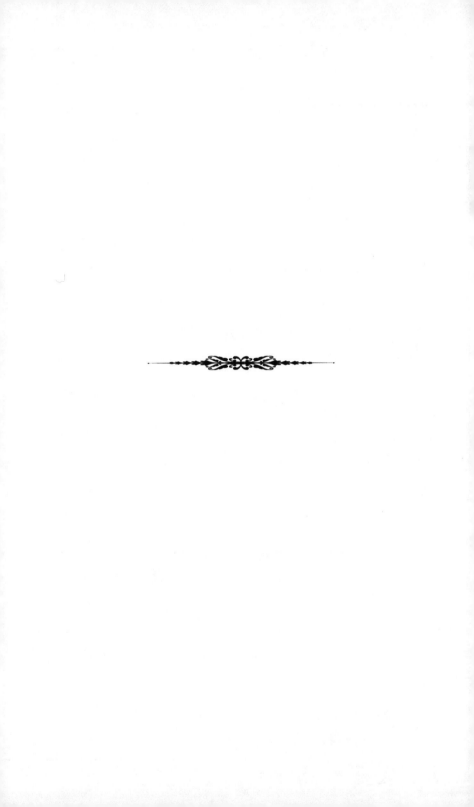

"To the artist is sometimes granted a sudden, TRANSIENT insight which serves in this matter for experience. A flash, and where previously the brain held a dead fact, the soul grasps a living truth! At moments we are all artists."

Arnold Bennett, English novelist

T

tableau *(tah-BLOW), noun*
A memorable scene created by the grouping of objects and people.
> *When Jeannette walked into the room, the TABLEAU of angry faces that greeted her revealed that we knew it was she who had gossiped to the society pages.*

tabula rasa *(TAB-yuh-luh-RAH-suh), noun*
A clean slate; lacking preconceived notions, prejudices, beliefs, and attitudes; receptive to instruction and information.
> *"Classic writer's fear of the blank page: call it TABULA RASA-phobia."* – John Jerome, American nonfiction writer

taciturn *(TAH-sih-turn), adjective*
Reserved; uncommunicative; a person of few words.
> *"Nature is garrulous to the point of confusion, let the artist be truly TACITURN."* – Paul Klee, German-born Swiss painter

tactile *(TACK-tile), adjective*
Related to the sense of touch.
> *This year's Parisian couture is distinguished by its use of highly TACTILE fabrics.*

tangential *(tan-JEHN-shull), adjective*
Divergent or digressive; having little to do with the subject or matter at hand.
> *"New York is full of people . . . with a feeling for the TANGENTIAL adventure, the risky adventure, the interlude that's not likely to end in any double-ring ceremony."* – Joan Didion, American journalist

tantamount *(TAN-tuh-mount), adjective*
Equivalent in value or effect.
> *Eleanor considered our snub of her TANTAMOUNT to betrayal and, in truth, she was correct.*

tantric *(TAN-trik), adjective*
Anything related to the school of thought that views sex as a sacred and deeply spiritual act.
> *"Both religions [Hinduism and Buddhism] were patronized by the same kings, ministers, and merchants, many of whom indulged in the same TANTRIC heterodoxies."* – William Dalrymple, Scottish historian and author

tautology *(taw-TAHL-uh-jee), noun*
A statement, principle, or phrase repeated many times in different ways for emphasis and resulting in redundancy.
> *After his wealthy father's death, Gerald consistently referred to his mother with the TAUTOLOGY, "widow woman."*

tawdry *(TAW-dree), adjective*
Gaudy, showy, and cheap, as clothes; or, base and mean, as motives.

T

> "Far from being the basis of the good society, the family, with its narrow privacy and **TAWDRY** secrets, is the source of all our discontents."
> *– Sir Edmund Leach, British author*

teem *(TEEM), verb*
To abound or swarm.
> *As we walked into the nightclub, the paparazzi TEEMED around us like so many manic worker bees.*

teleological *(tee-lee-uh-LOJ-ik-uhl), adjective*
The notion that things exist for a purpose.
> *The fact that we have unsurpassable wealth and taste, while others who are less important endure hardship, is surely proof that we live in a TELEOLOGICAL universe.*

temerity *(teh-MER-ih-tee), noun*
Possessing of boldness and confidence perhaps unwarranted by the situation at hand.
> *Anne, the girl who just moved to our gated community, had the TEMERITY to ask if we would invite her to one of our galas.*

temper *(TEHM-per), verb*
To moderate or lessen the impact of.
> *"Yet I shall TEMPER so / Justice with mercy." – John Milton, English poet*

temperance *(TEM-per-ance), noun*
Abstinence from consuming alcoholic beverages.
> *Cicero said that TEMPERANCE is "the firm and moderate dominion of reason over passion and other unrighteous impulses of the mind."*

tempestuous *(tem-PESS-chew-us), adjective*
Tumultuous and turbulent, as a personality.
> *Claire's TEMPESTUOUS personality is most likely linked to the fact that her father has married and remarried an excessive amount.*

temporal *(tem-PORE-uhl), adjective*
Relating to time.
> *"Science is the language of the TEMPORAL world; love is that of the spiritual world." – Honoré de Balzac, French novelist and playwright*

temporize *(TEHM-puh-rize), verb*
To gain time by being evasive or indecisive.
> *When an officious socialite tries to get too close to us, we do not feel the need to TEMPORIZE with our response; we simply remind her of her place.*

tenacious *(tuh-NAY-shuss), adjective*
Persistent, stubborn, obstinate.

> "Women are **TENACIOUS**, and all of them should be **TENACIOUS** of respect; without esteem they cannot exist; esteem is the first demand that they make of love." – *Honoré de Balzac, French novelist and playwright*

tendentious *(ten-DEN-she-us), adjective*
Describes statements or actions designed to promote one's beliefs or point of view.
> *Laura is TENDENTIOUS in her efforts to prove that she believes that a plentitude of fine jewelry is the key to happiness.*

tenebrous *(TEN-uh-bruss), adjective*
Dark and gloomy.
> *Eloise and Marcus spent the day exploring the TENEBROUS forest that surrounded their family's Maine compound.*

tenet *(TEH-net), noun*
A central philosophy; a core belief; a rule or principle one lives by.
> *"Christian writers from the third century on pointed out the deleterious effect of Platonism on Christian belief—even while adopting many of its fundamental TENETS." – Harold Attridge, Dean of Yale University Divinity School*

tenuous *(TEN-you-us), adjective*
Unsubstantiated and weak.
> *Roland's arguments to prove to us that it's better to give than to receive were TENUOUS at best.*

tepid *(TEHP-id), adjective*
Characterized by a lack of enthusiasm.
> *We greeted the new opera, with its mawkish plot and poor acting, with TEPID applause.*

tête-à-tête *(TET-ah-tet), noun*
A face-to-face meeting.
> *Some of us had begun to believe that our servants were pilfering from us, so we sat down the allegedly guilty parties and had a TÊTE-À-TÊTE.*

thaumaturge *(THAW-mah-turj), noun*
A person who works miracles.
> *If you were ever to see Hannah early in the morning, just after she has awoken, then you would know her personal make-up artist is the epitome of a THAUMATURGE.*

theocracy *(thee-AH-krah-see), noun*
A system of government in which priests rule in the name of God.
> *The Vatican is the ultimate THEOCRACY.*

tincture *(TINK-cherr), noun*
A trace amount or slight tinge.
> *The tragic opera was leavened with a TINCTURE of comic relief.*

titillate *(TIT-l-ate), verb*
To excite in an agreeable way.
> *With its stirring performance of Beethoven's Eroica Symphony, the full orchestra TITILLATED us at the Van Gelder's gala.*

titular *(TITCH-uh-luhr), adjective*
A person who is a leader by title only, but lacks any real power.
> *The Queen is the TITULAR head of the British empire.*

tombolo *(TOM-bo-low), noun*
A split that joins an offshore island to the mainland.
> *Until they decide to build a bridge, the single-lane road on the TOM-BOLO is the only way on to and off of the island.*

tome *(TOAM), noun*
A large or scholarly book.
> *"She carries a book but it is not / the TOME of the ancient wisdom, / the pages, I imagine, are the blank pages / of the unwritten volume of the new." – Hilda Doolittle, American poet and memoirist*

toothsome *(TOOTH-suhm), adjective*
Voluptuous and sexually alluring.
> *Dorienne is TOOTHSOME thanks mainly to her plastic surgeon and her family's attractive fortune.*

topical *(TOP-ih-kuhl), adjective*
Having to do with issues of current or local interest.
> *All the debutantes at the ball wasted our time with inane attempts at TOPICAL conversation about politics and other distasteful matters.*

topography *(tuh-POG-ruh-fee), noun*
The arrangement of the physical features of a place, area, or physical object; the "lay of the land."
> *After her return from Europe, Lauren spent most of her time talking about the dazzling alpine TOPOGRAPHY of Switzerland.*

torpor *(TORE-purr), noun*
Apathy; indifference.

> "A multitude of causes unknown to former times are now acting with a combined force to blunt the discriminating powers of the mind, and unfitting it for all voluntary exertion to reduce it to a state of almost savage **TORPOR**." – *William Wordsworth, British Romantic poet*

torrid *(TORE-ihd), adjective*
Ardent and passionate.
> *The TORRID romance between Alison and her family's stable boy lasted only a short time before the family discovered the tryst and fired the young man.*

tort *(TORT), noun*
In law, a civil misdeed requiring compensation of the victims.
> *Cutting the branches off a neighbor's tree that went over the fence into your yard is, at most, a TORT, not a felony.*

tortuous *(TORE-chew-us), adjective*
Intricate and indirect; not straightforward.

> "[Critics] don't know that it is hard to write a good play, and twice as hard and **TORTUOUS** to write a bad one." – *Anton Chekhov, Russian dramatist*

totem *(TOH-tuhm), noun*
Anything that serves as a venerated symbol.
Our various formal and informal gardens are TOTEMS to our emphasis on the importance of the natural world.

tout *(TOWT), verb*
To publicize in a boastful, extravagant manner.
Eloise TOUTED the excellence of her family's new personal chef to a gauche and distasteful degree.

tractable *(TRACK-tuh-bull), adjective*
Easy going; easily managed.
The occasional kind comment seems rather enough to keep our servants TRACTABLE.

tractate *(TRAK-tayt), noun*
A treatise.
Amanda's mother delivered a TRACTATE to her daughter about socializing with the right people after she learned that Amanda had been spending time with middle-class families.

traduce *(truh-DOOSS), verb*
To speak maliciously of; slander.
We have snubbed Katrina permanently because she has, at one time or another, TRADUCED each one of us in the society pages.

transcendent *(tran-SEN-dent), adjective*
Going beyond normal everyday experience; existing beyond the known physical universe and its limitations.
"Genius . . . means the TRANSCENDENT capacity of taking trouble."
– Thomas Carlyle, Scottish satirist and historian

transfiguration *(trans-fig-yuh-RAY-shun), noun*
An extreme change in appearance; a metamorphosis.
By the time of her coming out party, Brigitte had undergone a TRANS-FIGURATION from gawky child to poised and beautiful adolescent.

transgress *(trans-GRESS), verb*
To go beyond acceptable bounds.

> "Unjust laws exist; shall we be content to obey them, or shall we endeavor to amend them, and obey them until we have succeeded, or shall we **TRANSGRESS** them at once?" – *Henry David Thoreau, American author and transcendentalist*

transient *(TRAN-shunt), adjective*
Temporary; lacking permanence.
"To the artist is sometimes granted a sudden, TRANSIENT insight which serves in this matter for experience. A flash, and where previously the brain held a dead fact, the soul grasps a living truth! At moments we are all artists." – Arnold Bennett, English novelist

transmogrify *(trans-MOG-ruh-fie), verb*
To change appearance in a disturbing way.
We cannot abide that particular interior decorator because he always manages to TRANSMOGRIFY tasteful displays of luxury into pompous tableaus of arrogant wealth.

transubstantiation *(tran-sub-STAN-she-aye-shun), noun*
The notion of endowing something with symbolic value beyond its physical construct.
TRANSUBSTANTIATION is used as a technique in marketing, transforming shabby and gauche items into supposed examples of tasteful luxury.

travail *(truh-VAIL), noun, verb*
Pain and suffering due to a mental or physical hardship; or, to endure such pain and suffering.
Charlotte recently had to endure the TRAVAIL of going an entire week without her family's Olympic-sized swimming pool because the pool had developed a crack.

treacle *(TREE-kuhl), noun*
Contrived or mawkish sentimentality.
> *That writer's work is suffering in quality, as we could hardly sit through the TREACLE of her recently opened opera.*

tremulous *(TREHM-yuh-luss), adjective*
Timid and fearful.
> *With TREMULOUS mien, Anthony asked Gwendolyn if she would consent to a joining of their families.*

trenchant *(TREN-chunt), adjective*
Sarcastic; direct and to the point; intelligently analytical and accurate.
> *Michael's TRENCHANT commentary on American politics and society have made him a popular radio talk show host.*

triptych *(TRIP-tick), noun*
A picture or carving on three panels, or a set of three associated paintings or other works of art.
> *Scott wanted to buy just the center painting, but the gallery owner refused to break up the TRIPTYCH.*

Triton *(TRY-ton), noun*
A mythical creature, similar to a mermaid, with a human torso and arms, gills under the ears, and a tail like a dolphin.
> *TRITONS served Neptune as his attendants.*

troglodyte *(TRAHG-lah-dyte), noun*
A person considered to be primitive, out of date, coarse, uncouth, ill-mannered, or brutish.
> *Sick and tired of going out with TROGLODYTES, Janet told her friends she was through with blind dates.*

tropism *(TRO-prizm), noun*
The tendency of a plant or other organism to change direction in response to a stimulus; also used as a pejorative to describe reflexive or instinctual (i.e., mindless) human behavior.
> *The socialites demonstrate TROPISM as they flocked to the newly opened store of the newest high-fashion designer.*

truckle *(TRUHK-uhl), verb*
To submit obsequiously to a command.
> *We have trained our servants to TRUCKLE to our every whim.*

T

truculent *(TRUK-you-lent), adjective*
Belligerent; argumentative; always ready for a fight.
> *Short-tempered and TRUCULENT, Lucy could be set off by the slightest incident or comment.*

trumpery *(TRUHM-puh-ree), noun*
Something without value; a trifle.
> *The TRUMPERY that the Smythingtons collect and call "art" is, clearly, distasteful dreck.*

truncate *(TRUN-kate), verb*
To shorten something by cutting off the top or one of the ends.
> *Ellen looked ridiculous because she had chosen to TRUNCATE her floor-length party dress to tea-length hem.*

tryst *(TRIST), noun*
An appointment made by lovers to meet at a certain place and time.
> *Since their families are of equal station, no one worries much about the supposedly secret TRYSTS between Josephine and Brock.*

tumescent *(too-MESS-ent), adjective*
Becoming or already engorged, full, swollen, or rigid.
> *After the hurricane, our Florida compound was flooded by the TUMES-CENT intra-coastal waterway.*

tumid *(TOO-mid), adjective*
Pompous and swollen with pride.
> *We cannot stand it when Katherine wins arguments about couture and art collecting because the TUMID expression that crosses her face after a conversational victory is so loathsome.*

turgescent *(tur-JESS-ent), adjective*
Becoming or appearing swollen or distended.
> *His abs were so neglected, his stomach became TURGESCENT after a big meal.*

tyro *(TIE-roh), noun*
A beginner or novice.
> *Though a TYRO, Madeline quickly mastered cross-country skiing during her jaunt to Switzerland.*

"A gentleman doesn't pounce . . . he glides. If a woman sits on a piece of furniture which permits your sitting beside her, you are free to regard this as an invitation, though not an UNEQUIVOCAL one."

———

Quentin Crisp, British writer, actor, and model

ubiquitous *(you-BICK-wih-tuss), adjective*
Something that is everywhere, all around you, constantly surrounding you, and you cannot escape from it.

Wireless communication in the United States became UBIQUITOUS toward the close of the twentieth century.

ulterior *(uhl-TEER-ee-er), adjective*
Intentionally concealed, as motives.

"When one has extensively pondered about men, as a career or as a vocation, one sometimes feels nostalgic for primates. At least they do not have **ULTERIOR** motives." – *Albert Camus, Algerian-born French author and philosopher*

umbra *(UM-brah), noun*
A planet's shadow, especially the shadow of the Earth upon the moon.

A solar eclipse is caused by the Earth passing through the moon's UMBRA upon the sun.

umbrage *(UM-bridge), noun*
To take exception to and be offended by a comment or action seen as a slight or insult.

"I take UMBRAGE with people who post comments on my blog that are patently false," Bob said.

unassuming *(uhn-uh-SOOM-ing), adjective*
Modest and unpretentious.

The Binghamton's just bought a lovely, UNASSUMING 5,000 square-foot chalet in the Rockies.

unbridled *(un-BRY-duld), adjective*
Without limitations or boundaries; uncontrolled and unrestrained.

The customer's UNBRIDLED fury at being denied a refund was a sight to behold.

unceremonious *(un-sair-uh-MOAN-ee-us), adjective*
Discourteously abrupt, hasty, rude.

The maître d's UNCEREMONIOUS manner only made us love the new French restaurant all the more.

unctuous *(UNK-chew-us), adjective*
Possessing an untrustworthy or dubious nature; characterized by an insincere manner.
Local car dealers doing their own TV commercials often communicate in an UNCTUOUS, almost laughable manner.

undulate *(UN-jew-late), intransitive verb*
To move back and forth or from side to side in a smooth, slow motion.
Barbara and Bentley UNDULATED gracefully at their family's private ice rink.

unequivocal *(uhn-ih-KWIV-uh-kull), adjective*
Possessing a clear meaning or answer.
"A gentleman doesn't pounce . . . he glides. If a woman sits on a piece of furniture which permits your sitting beside her, you are free to regard this as an invitation, though not an UNEQUIVOCAL one." – Quentin Crisp, British writer, actor, and model

ungainly *(un-GAIN-lee), adjective*
Awkward and clumsy.
One of the hallmarks of this year's fashionable shoes is that they make one seem UNGAINLY on anything other than marble flooring.

uniformitarianism *(you-ni-form-ih-TARE-ee-uhn-izm), noun*
The belief that change on Earth takes place slowly, gradually, and at a uniform rate rather than through short, sudden, catastrophic events.
The fact that the families of our servants have been with us for many, many generations would seem to be proof of UNIFORMITARIANISM.

unilateral *(you-nhi-LAT-ur-uhl), adjective*
A decision that affects many people or states, but that is made independently by a single authority, without consulting those whom it affects.
We made a UNILATERAL decision to exclude Edwin from our group of possible paramours due to his distasteful habit of kissing and telling.

unimpeachable *(un-ihm-PEE-chuh-bull), adjective*
Above reproach; impossible to discredit or slander.
We promoted Carla to upstairs maid because her job performance has been UNIMPEACHABLE.

unitary *(YOU-ni-tare-ee), adjective*
A thing that exists or occurs in discrete units, sections, parts, or steps.
"*Today we can see life as a UNITARY process, made up of a number of smaller processes.*" – *Julian Huxley, English evolutionary biologist*

unsavory *(un-SAYV-err-ee), adjective*
Distasteful; unpleasant; disreputable; of dubious reputation.
"*Our future is inextricably linked to what happens in Washington DC, and we know that is a very UNSAVORY reality.*" – *Don Libey, direct marketing advisor*

unrenumerative *(un-re-NEW-mer-ah-tiv), adjective*
A job, investment, business venture, or other activity that pays little or no financial return.

"We find the wealth of our cities mingled with poverty and **UNRENUMERATIVE** toil." – *Grover Cleveland*

untenable *(uhn-TEN-uh-bull), adjective*
Not possible to defend, as an argument or position.
"*Are the legitimate compensation and honors that should come as the result of ability and merit to be denied on the UNTENABLE ground of sex aristocracy?*" – *Bertha Honore Potter Palmer, American socialite*

unwieldy *(un-WEEL-dee), adjective*
Not easy to handle or to manage.

"Now mark me how I will undo myself. / I give this heavy weight from off my head, / And this **UNWIELDY** sceptre from my hand, / The pride of kingly sway from out my heart." – *William Shakespeare*

upbraid *(up-BRAYD), verb*
To censure or to find fault with.
We had to UPBRAID our butler severely when we learned he was gossiping to other members of our staff.

urbane *(err-BANE), adjective*
Suave, sophisticated, refined, cosmopolitan, and well versed in the ways of high society.
Even in his knock-around tennis whites, Brett always manages to appear URBANE.

urbanization *(ur-ban-ih-ZAY-shun), noun*
The growth of cities brought about by a population shift from rural areas and small communities to larger ones.
URBANIZATION, which began in the United States in the late 1800s, was in part triggered by the shift from an agricultural economy to an industrial one.

usurper *(you-SIR-per), noun*
A person who seizes a position of power through illegal means, force, or deception.
"A USURPER in the guise of a benefactor is the enemy that we are now to encounter and overcome." – William Leggett, American poet and fiction writer

usury *(USE-err-ee), noun*
To charge illegally high or excessive interest rates on a loan.
Loan sharks lend money at USURIOUS rates, and break your legs if you don't make back the principal with interest on time.

utilitarian *(you-till-ih-TAYR-ee-an), adjective*
Showing preference for things and ideas that are practical and utterly pragmatic while eschewing the fanciful and useless.
Paul's UTILITARIAN mindset makes him an ideal trader on Wall Street.

utopia *(you-TOE-pee-uh), noun*
A perfect or ideal society.
Many of us who are accustomed to wealth have learned to accept that we must make our own UTOPIAS, rather than to rely on the actions of outside forces or agencies.

uxorious *(uhk-SAWR-ee-us), adjective*
Doting on one's wife to an excessive degree.

"The same things change their names at such a rate; / For instance— passion in a lover's glorious, / But in a husband is pronounced **UXORIOUS**." – *Lord Byron, British Romantic poet*

"One impulse from a VERNAL wood / May teach you more of man, / Of moral evil and of good, / Than all the sages can."

———

William Wordsworth, British Romantic poet

vacillate *(VAH-sill-ate), verb*
To swing back and forth between two points.
> *"But modern character is inconstant, divided, VACILLATING, lacking the stone-like certitude of archaic man. . . ." – Saul Bellow, American author*

vacuous *(VAK-yoo-us), adjective*
Devoid of emotion, intelligence, or any normal human thought processes; stupid; moronic.
> *The VACUOUS stare from her two eyes, looking like raisins pushed into a lump of dough, made him shiver with loathing and contempt.*

vagary *(VAY-guh-ree), noun*
A random or unexpected occurrence.
> *One needs to accept the VAGARIES of life if one is to be happy or at least content.*

vainglorious *(vayne-GLOR-ee-us), adjective*
Conceited; boastful; prone to showing off and bragging.
> *Although the scion of a well-established family, Gordon is so VAINGLORIOUS that you'd think him a parvenu!*

valuation *(val-you-AYE-shun), noun*
The calculated worth or value of an asset, based on a rigorous appraisal.
> *One of the accounting firm's services is business VALUATION, where you can pay to have an accurate appraisal of what your business would sell for if acquired.*

vanguard *(VAN-gard), noun*
That which is at the forefront or the leading edge; the most advanced group.
> *Robert is among the VANGUARD of area oenophiles.*

vapid *(VAH-pid), adjective*
Dull; void of intellectual curiosity or intelligence; lacking spirit and enthusiasm; dull, routine, unchallenging.
> *What irked him most about his sister-in-law was her VAPID stares in response to simple questions, conversation, and jokes.*

variegated *(VAIR-ee-ih-gate-ed), adjective*
That which changes color or contains different hues of the same color.
> *A lawn covered in VARIEGATED fallen leaves is the sign that autumn is finally here.*

vehement *(VEE-heh-ment), adjective*
Insistent; unyielding in one's opinion or decision; intense inflexibility about matters.

> *Milly, a chronic worry wart, was VEHEMENT about her children calling her if they were going to be late getting home from school.*

venal *(VEE-null), adjective*
Refers to people who can be bought, bribed, or otherwise persuaded to deviate from their beliefs and purpose.

> *"Give me but the liberty of the press, and I will give to the minister a VENAL House of Commons." – Richard Brinsley Sheridan, Irish playwright and statesman*

venerable *(VEN-err-uh-bull), adjective*
An individual or institution that is respected and revered, sometimes because of achievement, intelligence, or character; but just as often as a result of being around a long time.

> "Is the babe young? When I behold it, it seems more **VENERABLE** than the oldest man." – *Henry David Thoreau, American author and transcendentalist*

venial *(VEE-nee-ul), adjective*
A pardonable offense; a minor misdeed for which one is easily forgiven.

> *Cassidy was initially angry that Carley lied to her about where she bought her vintage handbag, but soon deemed the deed VENIAL.*

veracity *(ver-ASS-ih-tea), noun*
The characteristic or habit of being truthful and conforming to accepted standards of behavior.

> "The world is upheld by the **VERACITY** of good men: they make the earth wholesome." – *Ralph Waldo Emerson, American poet, essayist, and transcendentalist*

verbiage *(VER-bee-ij), noun*
Words; in particular, prose written to fill space and impress others rather than communicate ideas and information.

> *"There's some white space on the back page of the sales brochure," the marketing manager told his ad agency, "so let's fill it with some VER-BIAGE about service and quality."*

verbose *(ver-BOHS), adjective*
Describes a person or composition using more words than are needed to get the point across.

> *Long-winded and VERBOSE, Mitch made his team members groan whenever he stood up to speak at a charity event.*

verdant *(VUR-dant), adjective*
Lush with trees, bushes, ferns, and other green foliage.

> *With its careful mix of plants, the Whittingtons' formal garden remains VERDANT year-round.*

veritable *(VER-ih-tah-bull), adjective*
Genuine; the real thing; a perfect specimen or example.

> *"For me, the child is a VERITABLE image of becoming, of possibility, poised to reach towards what is not yet, towards a growing that cannot be predetermined or prescribed." – Maxine Greene, American philosopher and educator*

vernacular *(ver-NAK-you-lar), adjective, noun*
The language of a particular region or specific group of people.

> *Communicating with stockbrokers is difficult for many investors because they do not speak the VERNACULAR of the financial world.*

vernal *(VER-nul), adjective*
Related to spring.

> *"One impulse from a VERNAL wood / May teach you more of man, / Of moral evil and of good, / Than all the sages can." – William Wordsworth, British Romantic poet*

vers libre *(VERSS-LEE-breh), noun*
Free verse, a style of poetry requiring no rhyme or meter.

> *H. L. Mencken observed that VERS LIBRE is "a device for making poetry easier to write and harder to read."*

vertiginous *(ver-TIJ-uh-nuss), adjective*
Causing vertigo, imbalance, dizziness, or stumbling.
> *Mallory and Michael enjoyed their weekend getaway to Paris, spending many moments staring at the Parisian skyline from the VERTIGINOUS heights of the Eiffel Tower.*

vestigial *(VESS-tih-jee-ul), adjective*
Describes a remaining sample or trace of something that is disappearing or has already all but disappeared.
> *Some babies are born with a VESTIGIAL tail at the base of the spine.*

vexation *(vek-SAY-shin), noun*
Frustration, annoyance, or irritation resulting from some action, occurrence, or statement.
> *"There is not much less VEXATION in the government of a private family than in the managing of an entire state." – Michel de Montaigne, Renaissance scholar*

vicariously *(vye-KARE-ee-uss-lee), adverb*
To enjoy imagined feelings and experiences largely by observing or hearing about another person's life and adventures.
> *Married for over twenty-five years, Roger often told his single friends that he lived VICARIOUSLY through them.*

vicissitudes *(vi-SIS-ih-toods), noun*
The constant change of one's situation or condition, common throughout life.

> **"VICISSITUDES** of fortune, which spares neither man nor the proudest of his works, which buries empires and cities in a common grave."
> – *Edward Gibbon, British historian*

vignette *(vin-YET), noun*
A brief story, incident, or episode, usually told to illustrate some point.
> *Adding a VIGNETTE or two to a speech can help make abstract ideas clearer.*

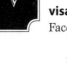

vindicate *(VIN-dih-kate), verb*
To prove your opinion is correct, or your action justified, or that you are innocent of a misdeed you stand accused of, despite opinions and evidence to the contrary.

We laughed at Paulette's predictions about the imminent fall fashions, but, once the couture was unveiled, Paulette was VINDICATED.

visage *(VIZ-aj), noun*
Face or overall appearance.

When the doctor entered the patient lounge, his grim VISAGE told the whole story before he could say a word.

visceral *(VIS-er-ul), adjective*
An immediate and strong gut reaction; a quickly formed opinion, based mainly on instinct and usually negative in nature.

"[Multiculturalism's] passions are political; its assumptions empirical; its conception of identities VISCERAL." – Joyce Appleby, American historian

vitriol *(vih-tree-AWL), noun*
An attitude of bitterness, hatred, or mean-spiritedness.

The school board reprimanded the coach with VITRIOL.

vituperative *(veye-TOO-pre-tiv), adjective*
A person who is bitter and angry, and readily takes that anger out on those around them.

VITUPERATIVE to an unreasonable degree, George smashed one of Jessica's prized dishes for every one of his old golf clubs she had given away when cleaning out the garage.

vivacious *(vy-VAY-shuss), adjective*
Joyful; happy, spirited; possessing a positive attitude about and enthusiasm for life; a person who lives life to the fullest.

Even after her family maintained some steep revenue losses, Sandra retained her VIVACIOUS character.

vociferous *(vo-SIF-er-uss), adjective*
Something said loudly so as to gain the listener's attention; a person who speaks loudly so as to gain attention.

"Let the singing singers / With vocal voices, most VOCIFEROUS, / In sweet vociferation out-vociferize / Even sound itself." – Henry Carey, English poet

volitional *(voe-LISH-uhn-uhl), adjective*
Describes an action performed or thought achieved through deliberate and conscious effort.

> *Our servants' persistent and VOLITIONAL attention to detail makes them absolutely indispensable to us.*

voluptuous *(vuh-LUP-chew-us), adjective*
Anything arising from or giving extreme sensory or sensual pleasure.

> *A VOLUPTUOUS banquet was the highlight of the Masterlys' Thanksgiving gala.*

voracious *(vo-RAY-shuss), adjective*
Possessing a huge and insatiable appetite, whether for food, knowledge, amusement, or something else.

> *Her son always had a VORACIOUS desire for knowledge. He read anything he could get his hands on and was always willing to experience something new.*

vortex *(VOR-teks), noun*
Liquid or gas swirling in a spiral that sucks everything in or near it toward its center; a problem or situation that draws in everyone around it.

> *The permanent whirlpool where the river goes underground is a dark VORTEX sucking in everything in its current.*

vox populi *(VOKS-pop-you-LYE), noun*
Expression of the prevailing mood, concerns, and opinions in a country.

> *In response to an environmentally friendly VOX POPULI, more and more corporations are "going green."*

"In our WANDERLUST, we are lovers looking for consummation."

Anatole Broyard, literary critic
for the *New York Times*

waft *(WAFT), verb*
To carry lightly, as if caught in a breeze.

> "This quiet sail is as a noiseless wing / To **WAFT** me from distraction."
> – *Lord Byron, British Romantic poet*

waggish *(WAG-ish), adjective*
Joking, witty, and mischievous.
> *"This species of 'fame' a WAGGISH acquaintance says can be manufactured to order, and sometimes is so manufactured."* – *Herman Melville, American author*

waif *(WAFE), noun*
A stray person or animal.
> *The occasional nouveau riche WAIF may float into our circle, but she rarely lasts long.*

wan *(WAHN), adjective*
Showing or suggesting ill health or unhappiness.
> *"So shaken as we are, so WAN with care, / Find we a time for frighted peace to pant."* – *William Shakespeare*

wanderlust *(WON-dehr-lust), noun*
A strong and innate desire to travel far from home.
> *"In our WANDERLUST, we are lovers looking for consummation."* – *Anatole Broyard, literary critic for the* New York Times

wane *(WAYN), verb*
To gradually decrease; to fade away; to become diminished.
> *Once she finally received the Cartier watch from her father, Karen's interest in the timepiece quickly WANED.*

wangle *(WANG-guhl), verb*
To accomplish by underhanded methods.
> *Jennifer managed to WANGLE an invitation to the Clarksons' party, even though she is the gauchest of the area's parvenus.*

wanton *(WAHN-tn), adjective*
Loose, lascivious, and lewd.
> *Robert is so WANTON that women stay away from him in spite of his family's connections.*

waspish *(WOS-pish), adjective*
Irascible and petulant; given to resentment.
Rebecca can be WASPISH, but we forgive her because she gives the best galas.

wassail *(WAH-sull), noun*
A salute or toast given when drinking to someone's health, well-being, or success.
We lost count of the mugs of beer consumed with the numerous WAS-SAILS to our teacher wishing him a happy retirement.

watershed *(WAW-ter-shed), noun*
An important event that signals the beginning of a new era or phase.
We knew it was a WATERSHED event when the Smythingtons did not hold their annual New Year's Eve gala last year.

watermark *(WAW-terr-mark), noun*
A faint design, graphic, or lettering pressed into paper while it is still in pulp form.
The CEO's classy letterhead bears a WATERMARK of the company logo.

wayfaring *(WAY-fair-ing), adjective*
Traveling on foot.
We spent many WAYFARING weekends during our month-long jaunt in France last year.

weal *(WEEL), noun*
Prosperous well-being; vitality.
Jordan is convinced that expensive jewelry is necessary for one's WEAL and welfare.

weir *(WEERE), noun*
A low dam or barrier built across a river either to control water levels or catch fish.
When the water level in the Passaic River lowered during a drought, a stone WEIR built by Indians for catching fish became visible.

weltschmerz *(VELT-schmayrtz), noun*
A lingering sorrow that some believe is a given in life.
When we snubbed Margaret for buying so many fashion knockoffs, her WELTSCHMERZ lasted until we forgave her.

wend *(WEND), verb*
To go; to proceed.

> "As they **WEND** away / A voice is heard singing / Of Kitty, or Katy, / As if the name meant once / All love, all beauty." – *Philip Larkin, British poet, novelist, and jazz critic*

whelp *(WEHLP), noun*
A despised person or his or her offspring.
> *"'Twas Slander filled her mouth with lying words, / Slander, the foulest WHELP of Sin." – Robert Pollok, Scottish poet*

wherewithal *(WAIR-with-all), noun*
Means or resources; money.
> *We certainly have the WHEREWITHAL to visit that restaurant, but we will not because the maître d' does not know his place.*

whimsical *(WIHM-zih-kuhl), adjective*
Erratic, unpredictable, capricious.
> *"How truly does this journal contain my real and undisguised thoughts— I always write it according to the humour I am in, and if a stranger was to think it worth reading, how capricious—insolent & WHIMSICAL I must appear!" – Frances Burney, British novelist, diarist, and playwright*

wily *(WHY-lee), adjective*
Crafty and cunning.
> *When it comes to parting Brock from his inheritance, the normally charming Mallory can be quite WILY.*

winnow *(WIN-oh), verb*
To find what one is looking for through a process of elimination in which many candidates are considered but only a few are chosen.
> *Selma WINNOWED through her wardrobe until she found the perfect Vera Wang gown to wear to the New Year's Eve ball.*

winsome *(WIN-suhm), adjective*
Winning and engaging; charming.
> *Lydia looked quite WINSOME throughout her coming out party.*

wistful *(WIHST-full), adjective*
Yearning, pensive; having an unfulfilled desire.

> "I never saw a man who looked / With such a **WISTFUL** eye / Upon that little tent of blue / Which prisoners call the sky." – *Oscar Wilde, Irish playwright and poet*

witticism *(WIT-uh-siz-uhm), noun*
A witty or clever remark.
> *We love our servants because they are so full of WITTICISMS about people of their class.*

wizened *(WIZ-uhnd), adjective*
Withered; shriveled; dried up
> *Moira spent so much time out in the sun during her Mediterranean trip that she came back positively WIZENED.*

wont *(WAWNT), adjective or noun*
Accustomed; or, a custom or practice.
> *"I am WONT to think that men are not so much the keepers of herds as herds are the keepers of men, the former are so much the freer." – Henry David Thoreau, American author and transcendentalist*

wrest *(REST), verb*
To pull away; to take something by force or threat.

> "**WREST** once the law to your authority: / To do a great right, do a little wrong." – *William Shakespeare*

wunderkind *(WUHN-der-kind), noun*
One who succeeds in business, or a similar endeavor, at a comparatively young age.
> *Alex would be a WUNDERKIND in the firm even without his father's connections.*

Such epithets, like pepper, / Give ZEST to what you write; / And, if you strew them sparely, / They whet the appetite: / But if you lay them on too thick, / You spoil the matter quite!""

Lewis Carroll, English author
and logician

X, Y, & Z

Xanadu *(ZAN-uh-dyoo), noun*
A place of perfect, idyllic beauty.

"In **XANADU** did Kubla Khan / A stately pleasure-dome decree: / Where Alph, the sacred river, ran / Through caverns measureless to man / Down to a sunless sea" – *Samuel Taylor Coleridge, English poet*

xanthic *(ZAN-thick), adjective*
Of a yellowish tint or color.
> *After Laura wore a XANTHIC dress to the spring ball, the area's nouveau riche followed her example at subsequent galas.*

Xanthippe *(zan-TIP-ee), noun*
An ill-tempered, shrewish woman.
> *Felicia is far from a XANTHIPPE simply because she interacts only with certain members of the household staff.*

xebec *(ZEE-beck), noun*
A small, three-masted ship used in the Mediterranean for commerce that once was a favorite vessel of the leisure class.
> *All of the amassed XEBECS ruined the otherwise spectacular views from our villa during the month we spent on the Greek Isles.*

xenocurrency *(zen-uh-KURR-uhn-see), noun*
Money that is circulated or traded in money markets outside its country of issue.
> *The Wallaces stopped speculating in XENOCURRENCY once rumors of a worldwide recession began circulating.*

xenogamy *(zih-NAHG-uh-me), noun*
Cross-pollination among plant species.
> *The secret of our award-winning formal gardens is the careful use of XENOGAMY.*

xenophile *(ZEN-uh-file), noun*
Someone who is attracted to foreign styles, customs, manners, etc.
> *All of us are XENOPHILES because American customs and cultural products are so gauche.*

xenophobic *(zee-nah-FOE-bik), adjective*
Having an irrational fear of foreigners and immigrants.
> *We are not XENOPHOBIC; we dislike all strangers, regardless of their backgrounds, unless they are brought to us by other social contacts.*

xenoplastic *(ZEN-uh-plass-tick), adjective*
Of, or occurring between, distantly related individuals.
> *We always have the senders of cards and letters carefully screened because some of us have been involved in XENOPLASTIC schemes by which total strangers suggested they belong to our family.*

xerochilia *(ZEER-uh-kile-ee-uh), noun*
Dryness of the lips.
> *Kyle may be cute, but the way he treats his chronic XEROCHILIA with common lip balm is nothing short of distasteful.*

xerophyte *(ZER-oh-fight), noun*
A cactus, succulent, or other plant that has adapted to living in a desert with limited rainfall or irritation.
> *We make use of a XEROPHYTE garden at our southwest desert estate.*

xerosis *(zih-ROH-sis), noun*
The typical hardening of aging skin and tissue.
> *Ophelia constantly visits European spas to slow the onset of XEROSIS.*

xiphoid *(ZIE-foid), adjective*
Shaped like a sword.
> *We can always spot Carlson's private plane because it is covered with the same XIPHOID shapes that adorn his family's crest.*

xylography *(zie-LAHG-ruh-fee), noun*
The art of engraving wood.
> *Even though it is not particularly valuable, we keep great-grandfather's XYLOGRAPHY collection because it meant something to him.*

yahoo *(YAH-hoo), noun*
A boorish, uncultivated, common person.
> *"Factory windows are always broken. / Somebody's always throwing bricks, / Somebody's always heaving cinders, / Playing ugly YAHOO tricks." – Vachel Lindsay, American poet*

yammer *(YAM-uhr)*, *verb*

To whine or complain loudly and at length.

The way Roland YAMMERS about being thrown out of Yale, you'd think he hadn't begged his father to make the expulsion happen!

yantra *(YAHN-truh)*, *noun*

A geometric diagram used to help one meditate.

During Eloise's foray into Buddhism, she kept forgetting her mantra, so her teacher gave her a YANTRA that she could affix to the wall in front of her meditation cushion.

yardarm *(YAHRD-arm)*, *noun*

Either of the outer portions of a square sail.

During the regatta, the yachts sailed YARDARM to YARDARM, appearing as though they may collide at any moment.

yare *(YARE)*, *adjective*

Quick and agile; lively.

Thanks to the gymnastics she performed at finishing school, Amanda has a YARE and limber body.

yaw *(YAW)*, *verb*

An erratic, side-to-side motion; or, to swerve.

A fast-moving cold front caused Sasha's Learjet 60 to YAW dangerously for several minutes.

yawnful *(YAWN-full)*, *adjective*

Arousing tedium or boredom.

Eleanor's YAWNFUL story about her month doing volunteer work made many of us bolt for the doors.

yawp *(YAWP)*, *noun, verb*

A raucous, clamorous noise; or, to make such a noise.

"I sound my barbaric **YAWP** over the roofs of the world." – *Walt Whitman, American poet and humanist*

yearling *(YEER-ling)*, *adjective or noun*

Of a year's duration; or, an animal in its second year.

Many of our family's racehorses are YEARLINGS, which we put to pasture after their retirement.

yen *(YEN), noun*
A strong desire or urge.
"Perhaps one subtext of the health care debate is a YEN to be treated like a whole person, not just an eye, an ear, a nose or a throat." – Anna Quindlen, American author and opinion columnist

yenta *(YEN-tuh), noun*
A woman considered a busybody or gossip.
Spreading rumors among ourselves is one thing, but Rebecca has gained a reputation as a YENTA because she also blabs to the help.

yeoman *(YOH-muhn), adjective, noun*
Pertaining to or one who performs arduous tasks in a loyal and work-manlike manner.
We promoted Helga to upstairs maid because of her YEOMAN work ethic.

yob *(YAHB), noun*
A cruel and loutish young man; a bully.
"Mick Jagger, alternately slurring YOB and lisping lordling, is classless-ness apotheosised." – Phillip Norman, British author

yokel *(YOH-kuhl), noun*
A gullible inhabitant of a rural area.
"[A human being] is the YOKEL par excellence, the booby unmatchable, the king dupe of the cosmos." – H. L. Mencken, American magazine editor, essayist, and critic

younker *(YAHN-kuhr), noun*
A young man or child.
Alex has been a fine horseman since he was a mere YOUNKER, playing with his family's thoroughbreds.

zabaglione *(zah-buhl-YOH-knee), noun*
An Italian dessert delicacy featuring a foamy, custard-like mix of egg yolks, sugar, and wine.
Even though the café has been discovered by the general public, we still go to it for its delectable ZABAGLIONE.

za-zen *(ZAH-ZEN), noun*
Meditation in a cross-legged posture.
Christopher has taken to practicing ZA-ZEN, but at heart, we know his goal is still acquisition of wealth and power, not personal enlightenment.

zeal *(ZEEL), noun*
Great enthusiasm and energy for a cause or activity.
> *"The living, vital truth of social and economic well-being will become a reality only through the ZEAL, courage, the non-compromising determination of intelligent minorities, and not through the mass." – Emma Goldman, Bolshevik anarchist*

zealot *(ZEL-it), noun*
A rabid follower; a true believer; a fanatical advocate.
> *"What a noble aim is that of the ZEALOT who tortures himself like a madman in order to desire nothing, love nothing, feel nothing, and who, if he succeeded, would end up a complete monster!" – Denis Diderot, French philosopher*

zeitgeist *(ZITE-gahyst), noun*
The prevailing viewpoints, attitudes, and beliefs of a given generation or period in history.
> *In the twenty-first century, "going green" is very much at the forefront of the nation's ZEITGEIST, as people have been made aware of the importance of being good stewards of our planet's natural resources.*

zelig *(ZEH-lig), noun*
A chameleonlike person who seems omnipresent.
> *The parvenus try so hard to be ZELIGS, blending in seamlessly at our functions, but we can always spot them for the intruders they are.*

zen *(ZEHN), verb*
Generally speaking, to figure out the answer to a difficult problem with a flash of sudden insight.
> *After days of indecision regarding which gala to attend on a particular night, Danielle managed to ZEN the answer and make her choice.*

zenith *(ZEE-nith), noun*
The highest point attained; the peak.
> *"This dead of midnight is the noon of thought, / And Wisdom mounts her ZENITH with the stars." - Anna Letitia Barbauld, English poet and children's author*

zephyr *(ZEFF-uhr), noun*
A gentle breeze.
> *"Soft is the strain when ZEPHYR gently blows, / And the smooth stream in smoother numbers flows." – Alexander Pope, British poet*

zest *(ZEHST)*, *noun*
Extreme enjoyment; a lust for life
> *"Such epithets, like pepper, / Give ZEST to what you write; / And, if you strew them sparely, / They whet the appetite: / But if you lay them on too thick, / You spoil the matter quite!"* – *Lewis Carroll, English author and logician*

Zionism *(ZYE-on-iz-um)*, *noun*
The modern political movement to establish a Jewish homeland in Palestine.
> *The Wasserstein's give charitably not only to the community, but also in support of ZIONISM because the family has many relatives living in Palestine.*

zonifugal *(zoh-niff-YOU-gull)*, *adjective*
Passing out of, or away from, a region.
> *Our multinational European jaunt contained many ZONIFUGAL changes that, often, caused us to feel disoriented.*

zonk *(ZAWNK)*, *verb*
To stun or stupefy.
> *We were positively ZONKED by Marie's choice of couture for the very important Sanderson gala.*

zoomorphic *(zoe-uh-MORE-fihk)*, *adjective*
Having the form of an animal.
> *The Rossington's formal garden is peppered with delightfully ZOOMORPHIC topiaries that seem to mix flora and fauna in equal measure.*

ABOUT THE AUTHOR

Bob Bly, who has taught writing as an adjunct professor at New York University, is a freelance copywriter. His clients include Lucent Technologies, PSE&G, IBM, Kiplinger, Boardroom, ITT Fluid Technology, Praxair, and Medical Economics.

McGraw-Hill calls Bob Bly "America's top copywriter." His awards include American Artists & Writers Institute's 2007 Copywriter of the Year, the Standard of Excellence Award from the Web Marketing Association, and a Gold Echo from the Direct Marketing Association.

Bob has written more than seventy books including *Careers for Writers* (McGraw-Hill/VGM) and *The Elements of Business Writing* (Alyn & Bacon). His articles have appeared in *Amtrak Express*, *Cosmopolitan*, *Early to Rise*, *Bits & Pieces for Salespeople*, *Successful Meetings*, *Writer's Digest,* and many other publications. He is a regular columnist for *Target Marketing* and *The Writer*.

Before becoming a freelance writer, Bob was the advertising manager of Koch Engineering and a technical writer for Westinghouse. He is a member of the Specialized Information Publishers Association, American Institute of Chemical Engineers, and the Business Marketing Association.

Bob has appeared as a guest on dozens of TV and radio shows including Bernard Meltzer, Bill Bresnan, CNBC, and CBS Hard

Copy. He holds a B.S. in chemical engineering from the University of Rochester. You can reach him at:

Bob Bly
22 E. Quackenbush Avenue
Dumont, NJ 07628
Phone: 201-385-1220
Fax: 201-385-1138
E-mail: *rwbly@bly.com*
Website: *www.bly.com*

INDEX

Acceptance, 92
Accounting, 106
Accusation, 172
Action, 176
Adjacent, 29
Advantage, 107
Advise, 52
Africa, 100
Agreeable, 28
Airy, 51
Alcohol, 199
Ancient, 79
Anger, 26, 220
Animal, 80, 81, 144, 224, 232, 235
Annoyance, 87
Answer, 211
Anxiety, 28, 165
Apathy, 202
Appearance, 220
Appetite, 221
Approval, 6, 8, 160
Arctic, 80

Argue, 165, 206
Arithmetic, 119
Arrogant, 147
Art, 99, 123, 126, 155
Artist, 142
Astronomy, 194
Attack, 87
Attribute, 88
Authority, 44, 79, 142, 160, 191,
    192, 211
Average, 119
Awkward, 211

Barrier, 225
Beast, 71
Beauty, 3, 17, 230
Beginner, 132, 206
Behavior, 36, 70, 76, 100, 125,
    146, 153, 155, 159, 160
Belief, 8, 38, 45, 53, 78, 88, 121,
    133, 145, 157, 158, 174, 174,
    182, 183, 193, 200, 217

Believer, 234
Bell, 99
Bible, 130
Biography, 76
Bird, 105, 111, 155
Bitter, 2
Bizarre, 192
Blame, 25, 88, 89
Boast, 19
Body, 110
Bombardment, 24
Bond, 89
Bonus, 105
Book, 17, 202
Boundary, 154
Breakable, 62
Breasts, 104
Breeze, 235
Bribe, 40
Building, 58
Burden, 144
Business, 116, 132, 143, 172, 227

Calm, 76
Cancer, 121
Candy, 118
Career, 153
Carry, 224
Category, 178
Celebration, 14
Chance, 62
Change, 204, 211, 219
Chaos, 48
Charity, 155
Charming, 226
Chat, 28
Child, 132, 233
Choice, 127
Choreography, 104
Chromosomes, 68
Church, 110

Cliché, 7, 19
Clothing, 16, 77, 170, 183
Cold, 67
Collateral, 82
Collection, 151
Color, 93, 119, 121, 216, 230
Command, 205
Common
    people, 79, 112
    person, 231
Competent, 97
Complain, 71, 154, 232
Compulsive, 152
Conceited, 216
Conclusion, 44
Conflict, 28, 170
Confine, 86
Connection, 132
Contradict, 15
Contrived, 58
Conversation, 150, 174
Convince, 92
Copied, 37
Cordiality, 47
Correct, 47, 175
Cows, 19
Crafty, 226
Creative, 36, 60
Creature, 99, 100, 107, 188, 205
Creditor, 108
Crime, 89
Critical, 82
Criticism, 6, 92, 175, 184
Cry, 104
Culture, 2, 51, 78, 155, 156
Custom, 76, 227, 230

Dam, 225
Danger, 183
Data, 47
Daylight, 40

Dead, 46, 125
Debt, 2, 108, 174
Deceit, 72
Decision, 211
Decrease, 224
Delay, 176
Demolish, 171
Design, 225
Desire, 11, 37, 97, 186, 224, 227, 233
Dessert, 233
Development, 88
Diagram, 232
Difficult, 2
Director, 98
Disapproval, 6, 36, 40, 174
Discovery, 37
Disease, 150, 151
Dishonesty, 92, 120
Dispute, 175
Disrespect, 182
Dissenting, 58
Distasteful, 6
Diversion, 39
Divide, 17
Document, 96
Domination, 78
Dormancy, 106
Drink, 2, 17, 29, 164, 192, 199, 225
Dull, 216
Duty, 144

Earth, 194, 210
Eat, 69
Economy, 69, 172
Edge, 154
Elimination, 226
Embarrass, 38
Emotion, 25, 30, 44, 118, 145, 216

Energy, 46, 48, 106, 234
Engraving, 231
Enjoyment, 235
Enthusiasm, 46, 53, 234
Environment, 179
Equivalent, 198
Erase, 44
Estate, 107
Etiquette, 36, 60
Event, 19, 225
Evidence, 82, 90, 158
Evil, 59, 131
Example, 166
Exception, 7
Excitement, 61, 63
Experience, 14, 203
Experimental, 10
Extrovert, 70

Fact, 35
Factor, 15
Failure, 86
Fair, 45
Fake, 50, 59
False, 87, 188
Familiar, 166
Family, 109
Fate, 99
Fatigue, 105
Fault, 212
Fear, 9, 20, 80, 164, 205, 231
Fearless, 34
Feeling, 39, 176
Flaw, 61
Food, 2, 49, 192
Force, 97, 227
Foreigners, 231
Foreign policy, 93
Frantic, 63
Funeral, 99
Future, 10

Gas, 221
Gaudy, 199
Generosity, 126
Gestures, 69
Gift, 40, 105, 106
Girl, 67
Goal, 63, 96, 117
God, 35, 151, 201
Gossip, 233
Government, 17, 105, 120, 201
Greed, 11, 44, 77, 171
Growth, 130, 160
Guilt, 63

Happiness, 14, 60
Hard-working, 144
Harm, 28, 35, 90, 96, 117, 154
Hate, 18, 48, 124, 220
Heal, 182
Health, 29, 182, 225
Heir, 184
Hermaphrodite, 6
Hiding, 141
Holiday, 100
Home, 155
Humiliation, 86
Humor, 97

Idea, 58, 130, 175, 182
Idle, 173
Illegal, 117, 175, 213
Illness, 29, 150
Ill will, 92
Important, 182
Incriminate, 89
Indicator, 15
Ineffective, 136
Inequality, 87
Inevitable, 89
Infer, 54
Inflexible, 79

Information, 78
Injury, 172
Innocence, 52
Insight, 49
Inspiration, 4
Insult, 153
Intelligence, 217
Interchangeable, 63
Interest, 155
Interruption, 79
Introduce, 91
Island, 201

Job, 186, 212
Joking, 224
Joy, 44, 45, 66, 220

Kindness, 11, 15, 16, 26, 116
Knowledge, 27, 50, 131, 146, 157

Language, 36, 108, 177, 218
Law, 98, 145, 159, 202
Lazy, 104
Leader, 157, 201
Legitimate, 18
Letter, 124
Libel, 24
Liberty, 116
Light, 133
List, 49
Loan, 82
Loyalty, 60
Luck, 4, 37
Lust, 28
Luxury, 193

Magic, 107
Man, 178, 183, 184, 233
Manner, 110, 122, 142, 146, 160
Manuscript, 150
Masculine, 6

Meaning, 5, 135, 211
Means, 226
Medical, 80
Meditate, 232, 233
Mediterranean, 66, 107, 230
Meeting, 201
Metal, 121
Metamorphosis, 204
Middle class, 18
Milk, 104
Miracles, 201
Mist, 52
Mistake, 46
Model, 52
Modest, 210
Money, 11, 44, 87, 121, 152, 155,
    226, 230
Mood, 30, 221
Moon, 108, 194
Moral code, 14
Muscles, 99
Music, 25, 119, 193
Mysterious, 8, 48, 90

Name, 8
Nationalism, 97
Negative, 125
Neuter, 6
Noise, 232
North Pole, 81
Novel, 17

Occupation, 122
Offense, 61
Offensive, 142, 210
Opinion, 91, 141, 144, 145, 157,
    220
Optimism, 119
Ordinary, 134
Organize, 70
Over-exaggeration, 81

Ownership, 159
Oxygen, 147

Pain, 189, 204
Paralyze, 69
Passionate, 202
Payment, 174
Peak, 234
Persistent, 9
Person, 6, 9, 10, 14, 18, 19, 24, 25,
    27, 28, 35, 38, 40, 48, 60, 70,
    76, 77, 78, 80, 81, 86, 91, 97,
    104, 105, 108, 110, 111, 118,
    123, 134, 135, 143, 153, 154,
    155, 156, 165, 166, 175, 184,
    193, 198, 210, 205, 213, 218,
    220, 224, 226, 231, 234
Persuasion, 96
Philosophy, 119, 134, 200
Picture, 49, 205
Plan, 20
Planet, 151, 154, 186, 210
Plant, 144, 205, 230, 231
Playful, 66
Poetry, 99, 218
Politics, 35, 134
Pompous, 70
Poor, 87
Power, 142, 171, 191, 213
Pragmatic, 213
Praise, 3, 47, 53, 121
Precaution, 25
Predicament, 86
Prejudice, 96
Pretend, 161
Pride, 81, 206
Pristine, 93
Prize, 161
Problem, 151, 164, 171
Proceed, 226
Profession, 122

Pronunciation, 51
Property, 67, 82, 142
Prudent, 26
Publicize, 203
Purification, 112
Purpose, 199

Quiet, 190

Rage, 7
Random, 216
Real, 218
Reason, 170
Reflex, 173
Regret, 178
Religion, 24, 51, 69, 78, 110, 125,
  151, 155, 182, 185
Remark, 66
Reply, 173, 177, 178
Respect, 80, 140, 217
Rest, 165, 175
Reward, 80, 111, 121
Right, 39
Romantic, 179
Rouse, 62
Rude, 210
Rules, 27
Run, 66

Salute, 225
Salvation, 69
Sarcasm, 183
Satire, 105
Science, 99
School, 112
Sea level, 51
Secret, 192
Sect, 184
Segregation, 7
Self-contained, 90
Sentimental, 118, 205

Sex, 5, 61, 106, 108, 135, 182, 198
Ship, 230
Shy, 59
Size, 19
Slander, 24, 203
Small, 109
Smell, 142, 143
Snobbish, 77
Society, 14, 34, 77, 78, 109, 124,
  159, 160, 213
Solution, 135, 150, 171
Sorrow, 225
Sound, 156, 187, 192
South Africa, 7
Spacious, 27
Speak, 18, 38, 69, 110, 203
Spectrum, 67
Speech, 38, 46, 49, 61, 96, 119,
  156, 159, 193
Spine, 100
Steady, 50
Steep, 158
Story, 5, 7, 15, 19, 170, 219
Strange, 8
Strength, 145, 150
Stress, 50
Stubborn, 91, 200
Stun, 235
Success, 186, 227
Surrender, 24
Surroundings, 122
Swerve, 232
Symbol, 203

Talk, 37, 111, 140, 157
Taste, 71
Teacher, 152
Teasing, 170
Technology, 111
Temperament, 18
Temperature, 98